Trouble's Tales

The First Laugh

Humor, Heart, and the Occasional Disaster

Trouble's Tales: The First Laugh
Book One of the *Trouble's Tales* series
Told, and occasionally exaggerated, by Trouble Nigro

This book is a work of creative nonfiction, drawn from memory, mischief, and lived experience. Some details have been polished, bent, or lovingly reimagined, but the heart of each story is true. Names and identifying details may have been changed to protect privacy.

For permissions, inquiries, or correspondence, please contact: **natalie@presstrouble.com**

Illustrations are inspired by the spirit of Norman Rockwell, filtered through a life that can't help but turn the ordinary into something worth remembering.

ISBN: 979-8-9947002-0-4
Paperback format
First edition, 2026.

"Thanks for stepping into my stories. Life is serious enough. These pages are for the laughs, the gasps, and the memories that make us who we are."

DEDICATION

For Natalie
by Trouble (with a little help from her shadow poet)

I wrote these words with wrinkled hands,
Through memory's maze, through shifting sands.
Each line a thread from years gone by—
A laugh, a tear, a stubborn cry.

You've been the spark behind each page,
The reason wisdom met the stage.
When times got louder, days got strange,
You helped me bend, adapt, and change.

You listened close and laughed in sync,
You knew the story 'fore the ink.
You held the past with gentle care,
And nudged me on when I would stare.

You've helped me gather, sort, and tell,
The tales I'd lost or hid too well.
You gave me space to trip and try—
And caught my words when they would fly.

So here's my heart, in paper form,
These stories worn and true and warm.
You've made this book a sacred thing—
A quilt of life, with every string.

And when the day is far and wide,
And I'm no longer by your side,
Just open here and find me still,
With ink-stained fingers, loud goodwill.

Love you more than words allow—
From trouble then…
To your Trouble now.

Acknowledgments

This little book may have my name on the cover, but it was built with Natalie on shared stories, a lot of laughter, and more than one "wait, what were we talking about?"

To my daughter Natalie — who always is my tech support, editor, co-pilot, and emotional support human all in one — I couldn't have done this without her brain, her heart, and her infinite patience for my rabbit trails and storytelling detours.

To everyone who ever said, "You should write a book" this one's for you. I didn't write it to get famous (but hey, I'm not opposed), I wrote it because the stories wouldn't leave me alone. And because maybe, just maybe, you needed a laugh, a memory, or a little reminder that you're not the only one out here winging it.

To the strangers who became friends, the family who became characters, and the animals who became legends — thank you for making our lives stories worth telling.

Here's to all of you. Thank you for helping me remember, reflect, and, let's be honest, for letting me run my mouth one more time.

With gratitude (and probably a typo or two).

Memories don't fade.
They just get funnier,
louder, and more
exaggerated with time.
Thanks for letting
me share mine.

INTRODUCTION

If you've found your way to this book, welcome. Maybe someone handed it to you and said, "You've gotta read this woman—she's a hoot," or maybe you're just nosey, or you have heard one of my stories. Either way, glad you're here.

In case we haven't met, I'm Trouble, seventy-nine years young and still poking around in the business of memories, laughter, and the occasional existential pothole. My daughter Natalie and I have been having those late-night, big life, "what really matters" talks lately. The kind that shows up when life starts shifting, when the body gets a little slower and louder, and the future gets a little quieter.

Somewhere between a conversation and a confession, I realized: the best gift I can leave behind isn't a box of old photographs or a kitchen drawer full of mismatched utensils. It's my stories.

So, I started writing them down, not just for me, but for her. For the people I've met. For anyone who's ever said, "You should write a book." Now, let me tell you, every time someone said that, my answer was always, "No way. I've done that kind of thing before. It takes too much commitment, and too much organization — there's no way I'm writing a book." (Note to self: never say never again.) But mostly, I did it for Natalie, so that long after I'm gone — or worse, forgetful, she can crack open a page and find me there, laughing at my own stories.

This isn't just a collection of tales. It's a keepsake. It's a time capsule. It's therapy. And if I do it right, it'll make you laugh, cry, reflect, and maybe even realize that memories can be a blast.

Now is a pretty special time in my life. I get to slow down and speed up at the same time, reliving the moments that shaped me while creating something that might outlast me.

So, settle in. Let me tell you a story or two.

With love,

TROUBLE

TABLE OF CONTENTS

How Trouble Became "Trouble" 2
Hello Hamper 4
What a Way to Travel 6
Things Dogs Eat 8
Heck of a Question Before Coffee 10
Scooter, the Bone, and the Map King 12
A Backhoe and a Woman 16
Campfire and Marshmallows 18
What's in a Name? 20
Do Re Mi 22
Parade of Kitchens 24
From Pearls to Plaid 26
When the Walls were Paper 28
Financial Shock Therapy 30
Sandstone, Shutter Clicks, and Shenanigans 34
The Scanner Hates Me 36
Today, I got my "Flipper!" 38
What Happened to My Nickel? 40
A Lesson on the Rocks 42
3 Big Pigs 44
The Night I Attacked the Captain 46
Tools, Kids, and a Poem 48
Naughty Ornament Incident 56
Uninvited and Unstoppable 58
Fowl Play at Sunrise 60

Where Trouble Gets Caught 62
Low Bar, Cleared with Style 68
Snow Job 70
The Day We Googled 'Sex Bolt' 72
Catch This! 74
A Kiss for Christmas 76
Marinara, Musicals, and a Mormon 78
Do You Do Everything Your Mother Taught You? 82
Minor Incident Involving Panic 84
Dad in the Speaker 86
Earthquake at the Worst Time 88
Floods, Sandbags & Helicopters 90
A Roadside Dip to Remember 92
What'd you do that for? 94
Cheeky Business in Italy 98
Angels Among Us 100
Ginger Ale Geyser Games 102
When Masonry Meets Mayhem 104
Do Not Make Me Come Down There 106
Finding My Second Voice 110
Trouble, Tools, and Terrible Ideas 112
Mangia Till You Drop 114
Barefoot Days and Ice Cream Dreams 116
First Born, My Foot 118
Cherry Days, Rooftop Ways 120
A Lesson in Expectations 122
Florida Girl Meets the Japanese Alps 124
Rule-Breaking Librarian 128

Cutting Edge, Old School 130
Goat in the Chain Link Fence 132
Beneath a Blackened Sky 134
Raised Three, Kept Two More 136
Sushi and a Blunt Force Trauma 138
Thank you Scribbles 140

How Trouble Became "Trouble"

Most people don't know my real name, and honestly, I'm just fine with that. These days, I go by *Trouble*. Now, Facebook doesn't allow nicknames when you sign up. No flair, no sass, just your "government name." So, if you've found me there, you might see a name that doesn't quite match the mischief.

To help you make the connection, here's a little hint:

"I am known as Trouble, though some folks call me Shirley. Surely, I must be Trouble!"

So, how did I get that name?

Well, growing up, school wasn't always easy. Reading, in particular, gave me a real run for my money. Back then, they'd make us sit in a circle and read aloud, one by one. That circle felt more like a spotlight, and when it was my turn, the words on the page would just scramble themselves silly. I'd stumble, pause, guess, and more often than not, get it wrong.

The other kids? Oh, they'd laugh. Not the warm kind, either. So, I made a choice. If they were going to laugh anyway, I'd be the reason they laughed, but I'd make it on my terms. I started slipping in jokes and adding a little flair to my fumbles. Before long, the laughter wasn't mean anymore. It was shared. And for the first time, I felt like I had some control over it.

Turns out, that little survival tactic became a lifelong calling.

By the time I hit adulthood, people weren't teasing me anymore. They were greeting me with a grin and a cheerful, "Here comes Trouble!" And I loved it.

When I turned 65, something inside me just clicked. I realized that what I'd been doing all my life, making people laugh, connecting through humor, wasn't just a habit. It was a precious gift. So, I made a decision that day. From then on, I would introduce myself as "Trouble," and I would speak to as many individuals as possible: strangers, cashiers, waitresses, folks in line, anyone within earshot, and try to make them smile. Or laugh. Either one counted. Anything less just wasn't acceptable.

Now, at 79, I still lead with it. When I introduce myself and say, "Hi, I'm Trouble," something shifts. It opens a door, not just to conversation, but to joy. It lowers walls. People soften. They share. They laugh. And best of all, I learn.

I've heard beautiful, funny, heartbreaking stories from strangers I never would have met otherwise. The world doesn't always make space for joy, but I do. One grin at a time.

And let me tell you, being Trouble has never felt more right.

"When life hands you a nickname, turn it into your purpose in life."

HELLO HAMPER

One morning, as I went about my usual morning routine, I headed for our only bathroom which was surprisingly small for a household throne room. The mirror was already fogged from someone's shower, the faucet gave its steady *drip... drip...*, and a towel dangled halfway off its hook.

I had just picked up my toothbrush when I heard a faint sound. It was so soft, I almost didn't notice it. I froze, head tilted, listening. Nothing. Just the drip from the leaky faucet. Shrugging it off, I carried on brushing.

Then I heard it again. Something was going on, and I was determined to get to the bottom of it. Taking a leap into what I figured might be absurdity, I asked, "Is anyone there?" Crazy question, really. Our bathroom was the size of a closet, and I could see every inch of it. Surely, no one could hide here without me noticing.

To my absolute shock, a tiny voice answered, "Yes, it's me!" I froze, toothbrush mid-air, and looked around. Nothing. Maybe I was dreaming, or sleepwalking so I pinched myself. No, I was awake. The voice hadn't come from the air vents or a window. No, it was coming from... our laundry hamper.

Curiosity and mischief got the better of me. "What's your name?" I asked, trying to keep a straight face. "My name's Ham," the voice replied. "Well, hello, Ham," I said, stifling a chuckle. "How are you today?"

And just like that, I found myself having a full-blown conversation with a laundry hamper. It didn't take long for me to figure out what was really going on. My youngest had climbed into the hamper, likely playing hide-and-seek with his siblings. But did I let on that I knew? Oh, no. Opportunity had knocked, and I wasn't about to let it slip away.

Every morning for the next couple of weeks, I looked forward to waking up. I couldn't wait to exchange pleasantries with Ham while brushing my teeth. It became our little ritual, a whimsical start to my day that made me smile long after I left the bathroom. I felt like a kid again who had found a new friend.

But as with all things, the game eventually came to an end. One morning, Ham didn't answer. My youngest had moved on, as children do, leaving the hamper empty and silent.

I never confessed I knew it was him. Kids need secrets like those little mysteries they think they've pulled off, little games that remind them the world is a place of surprise. And to be honest, I needed it too, maybe more than he did. Life can get so loud, but those few silly minutes in the morning? They felt like a whisper from something bigger saying "You're doing just fine."

I missed those conversations, but I knew it was just another price to pay for watching my children grow up. One day they're hiding in hampers, and the next, they're too big for such antics. Still, I'll always remember my good friend Ham. And if I ever hear a faint voice from the hamper again, I'll know exactly what to say.

"Hello, Ham. It's good to see you again."

"If your laundry isn't talking to you, are you even parenting right?"

What a Way to Travel

Back when the kids were still knee-high and full of energy and noise, one summer, we decided to attempt camping somewhere in the Italian countryside.

Now, keep in mind, we had a Volkswagen hatchback. Not a van. Not an RV. A hatchback. And since we had three kids, we also had an au pair with us.

If you're wondering, "What in the world is an au pair?" let me help you out. It's a young adult, usually between 18 and 30, who lives with a host family in a foreign country. They help out with the kids and some light chores in exchange for room, board, and spending money. Kind of like a Mary Poppins on a budget, but with a passport.

Anyway, she came along for the ride and to help keep the kids under control. That meant three adults and three kids packed into that little German clown car.

Back then, cars didn't have air conditioning. Our cooling system was the open windows, and the warm wind would whip through the car while the road noise drummed along like background music.

The drive took hours. Only two people could sit in front, so I climbed in the back with the kids with all the camping essentials. Plus, a guitar, of course. You need a guitar for singing around the campfire. After all, the family that sings together stays together, even if we sang badly. Camping with young kids is a bit like moving cross-country: you need everything but the kitchen sink.

Eventually, the motion of the road and the boredom of the journey caught up with us, and we all did the natural thing—passed out cold. I mean, out like a light. We became a warm, tangled pile of limbs, mismatched socks, and dreams.

At one of the rest stops, my husband, bless his restless legs, got out to stretch and, seeing this ridiculous pile of humanity among all our camping junk, decided to snap a photo.

I swear, if he'd told me we all fit like that, I wouldn't have believed him. And yet, there we were—snoring in stereo, wrapped in towels and jackets, looking like we were auditioning for some kind of avant-garde family sculpture.

When we arrived at the campgrounds, it turned out to be a disaster. It was a massive mosquito breeding ground with no other campers there. We were going to be the main course for millions of them to feast upon.

Needless to say, we decided to pack it in and head home vowing that next time, we'd travel in style.

"Somewhere in Italy, this was luxury travel on a budget— and we were livin' the dream."

Things Dogs Eat

I was scrolling through social media the other day when I came across someone asking how to stop their dog from eating other dogs' poop. They were even looking for a pill to make the poop taste bad. Now, someone replied with the most honest question I've ever seen: "Doesn't poop naturally taste bad?!"

That sent me straight into a fit of laughter, and straight down memory lane to my own dog. Max was a beagle with a big personality and an even bigger appetite for… paper. Yup. Paper. You'd think a creature that could sniff out bacon from two blocks away would have better taste. But no, Max was a connoisseur of stationery.

One afternoon, a friend dropped by and asked, "What's Max's favorite treat?" Without missing a beat, I said, "Paper."

Thinking I was joking, my friend grinned, pulled a pad of Post-it notes from his bag, peeled one off, and offered it to Max. Max's tail started wagging so hard his whole backside danced. He gobbled it down with the satisfaction of someone who'd just discovered fine dining.

That was all the encouragement my friend needed. He peeled another one, then another, each time laughing harder as Max begged with those classic, heart-melting beagle eyes. You could practically hear Max saying, *"Please, sir, just one more."*

Before long, my friend was hand-feeding him little yellow squares like hors d'oeuvres at a cocktail party. And Max was loving every second.

I hated to break up their fun, but I finally had to step in before my yard turned into a paper mache exhibit the next day. After all, paper in… eventually means paper out, and nobody was ready for that part of the story.

But the best Max story? That would be the infamous check incident. By then, I was running my graphic design business. Max came to work with me most days, snoozing under my desk or charming clients who stopped by. One afternoon, a client dropped off payment by check. I placed it neatly on my desk, turned my back for all of thirty seconds, and when I looked again… it was gone.

Gone.

Max sat there, looking guilty and slightly smug, a little corner of the check sticking out from his mouth like a victory flag.

I had to make one of the strangest business calls of my career. I phoned a brand-new client and, trying to sound professional, calmly explained that my dog had eaten their payment.

Silence. Then a cautious, "He what?"

"Yes," I said. "Literally. Ate. Your. Check."

I tried to reassure them. "This isn't like a kid saying the dog ate their homework. Max actually ate it." Then, like a true fool, I even offered to mail them the, um… processed remains. They politely declined and simply mailed a replacement.

What can I say? Dogs are weird. Loyal, loving, soft-eared weirdos with bottomless stomachs and terrible judgment. But even when they eat something they shouldn't, they still manage to snuggle their way right into your heart.

"I could've sent the check back… but you wouldn't have wanted it."

HECK OF A QUESTION BEFORE COFFEE

There's nothing quite like being asked a brain-bending question before you've had your coffee, especially when the air still smells like toast, and your eyes aren't even fully open yet.

One morning, my 15-month-old toddled into the kitchen and, with the calm confidence of someone twice my age, asked: "Is today yesterday's tomorrow?"

Now this wasn't a babble or a fluke. This child spoke in full sentences, had been doing so for months, and had a habit of catching me off guard. But this question? This one scrambled my brain before the day had even started.

I just stood there, blinking at him, coffee pot in one hand, calendar flipping through my head like it was on fast-forward. Yesterday… today… tomorrow… wait, what day is it again? After a moment, I took a breath and gave him my answer.

What do you think I said? No, yes or I don't know? If you guessed yes, give yourself a gold star and pour a fresh cup of coffee. But the question lingered. Was he right? Is today yesterday's tomorrow? Well… yes. Yes, it is.

Just like that, my barely-a-toddler son had laid out a perfectly logical, time-centered riddle that made me stop in my tracks.

Looking back, it wasn't just cute or clever, it was exactly the kind of insight that came naturally to him. From a very young age, he noticed patterns, asked precise questions, and strung together ideas that made people look twice. He wasn't trying to be profound; he was just being himself... very curious, clear and smart.

And while I wasn't ready to debate the flow of time before breakfast, I'm glad he was. Because that moment reminded me of something we all forget: kids live in time, but they don't get stuck in it. They don't dwell on yesterday, and they don't worry about tomorrow. They just ask what matters now.

And maybe, just maybe, that's the kind of brilliance we all need a little more of.

So, if someone ever hits you with a cosmic-level question before your first sip of coffee, lean in. You might be talking to a sharp little soul who sees the world more clearly than the rest of us do.

And maybe that's the real magic of it all—kids remind us that the world still holds questions worth pausing for. Even now, at 79, I still have to stop and think before I can tell this story right.

"Some kids build towers. Mine built time theories."

SCOOTER, THE BONE, AND THE MAP KING

After my divorce, we weren't just leaving South Carolina, we were leaving a whole life behind. I didn't know exactly where we'd land, but I knew it wouldn't be here. I was 32 years old with three kids and no money. But I had one mission: start over.

I gave the kids a choice, something they rarely had while we bounced from one military base to the next. The options were Malibu, California (beautiful and wildly unrealistic), or Ogden, Utah (affordable, full of Mormons, and home to my sister, which meant at least one friendly face at the finish line). I wasn't religious, not in any organized way, but I respected faith in all its many flavors. I'd lived among Baptists, Catholics, and Jews without incident. Living in Utah didn't scare me. Starting over did.

We had a very democratic moment where each kid got a voice. Natalie voted for anywhere with snow, Todd wanted mountains, and Kirk wanted to know if hamburgers existed west of the Mississippi. Ogden it was.

So, we packed up what little we had left. Everything that didn't fit in the Dodge van was sold, donated, or abandoned to fate. The van ended up crammed with various essentials, clothes, sleeping bags, one tent, three kids, and Scooter.

She was a little black terrier mutt with low charm, low loyalty, and inexplicably high seniority. Full of nervous energy and a streak of pure chaos, she was not the ideal road-trip companion. But she was familiar, she was small, and she was the last remaining scrap of our "before" life.

Nobody liked her much. She wasn't likable, reliable, or particularly bright, but she was ours. A tiny, scruffy reminder that we had a past and we were dragging it—literally—into our future.

So, we hit the road.

No hotels. No motels. No money for any of it. Just a camping tent, and a few sleeping bags: we were going to "rough it".

This was 1979, which meant no GPS, no smartphone, and no soothing voice to "recalculate." All we had was a Rand McNally atlas the size of a cafeteria tray and Todd, my nine-year old who declared himself the Map King and clutched that atlas like scripture. He read maps like bedtime stories. You could ask him where Kansas was and he'd tell you the interstate numbers, the mileage between exits, the elevation change, three "better routes," and whether the gas stations leaned toward Pepsi or Coke (only that last one is an exaggeration).

And because he was the map reader, he got the front seat. This wasn't luxury; this was practicality. The other two kids stretched across our belongings like little human lasagnas.

Todd didn't earn his seat with charm. He earned it with accuracy, a ruler, and the bladder endurance of a drill sergeant.

His goal was simple: get there as fast as possible. My goal was even simpler: stay alive. These were not always compatible.

Todd's idea of fun was pushing us to drive twelve or thirteen hours straight. I was the only driver. No shifts. No naps. No cruise control. Just me, white-knuckling my way across America while Todd announced mileage like a caffeinated air-traffic controller. When I was about ready to throw the steering wheel out the window, magically, suddenly, a campground would appear. The boy had a sixth sense for the edge of my patience.

Camping with three kids and a dog after twelve hours of driving was a feat of military-grade logistics. We'd pull in after dark, dead tired, kids half asleep, me with one eye open. I'd pitch the tent with one hand, swat mosquitoes with the other, and pray nobody cried or bled.

Here's where the campgrounds added their own charm. Every place had a "welcome committee." Sometimes it was a swarm of bugs big enough to request their own tent. Sometimes it was a chatty neighbor with a lantern who materialized out of the shadows to critique our tent placement. Sometimes it was a man in a fishing hat who delivered unsolicited weather predictions with the confidence of a retired meteorologist.

And then… there was Scooter.

One night, that little menace trotted right into the campsite next to us and started digging like she was mining for gold. Before I could chase her down, she surfaced with a stranger's damp sock flapping from her jaws. I did what any single mother with shredded dignity would do. I looked away. Pretended not to know her.

The kids, of course, ruined everything by shouting, "SCOOTER, DROP IT!" loud enough to wake wildlife in three and a half counties.

After stunts like that, giving her the bone each night felt like handing a toddler a coloring book just to keep them occupied.

Her favorite thing? Burying that same stupid bone. Every. Single. Night. She'd trot off like she was running a covert mission for the CIA, hide her treasure, then strut back looking smug and dusty. No problem. Until morning.

Come sunrise, Scooter turned into a panicked archaeologist. She'd dig up every square inch of the campsite looking for the bone she herself buried. Yapping, sniffing, kicking up dirt like she was searching for buried treasure and her will to live. That dog couldn't find her own tail, let alone a buried bone.

The kids thought it was hilarious. They'd bet on where she'd find it next, cheering her on like it was the Kentucky Derby. Sometimes she unearthed the wrong thing—a stranger's flip-flop, a forgotten marshmallow stick—and paraded it triumphantly. I just sat with my instant coffee, equal parts admiration and exhaustion.

But the worst part wasn't the bone. Oh no. The worst part was Keep-Away.

We'd be packed up, van loaded, kids barely conscious in the back, and Scooter would look me dead in the eye… and bolt. Tail high. Ears back. Smiling. SMILING.

We'd call, chase, beg. She mocked us.

One morning, I snapped. "I'm leaving her," I said. "That's it. We're done."

Immediately, all three kids burst into tears.

"We can't leave Scooter! She's all we have left of our past life! You said we were a team!"

Let me tell you, nothing brings out raw emotion like sleep deprivation, cross-country fear, and a dog with commitment issues.

So, I got in the van. I started the engine. I eased forward.

Scooter saw the van move. And just like that, game over. She came sprinting, ears flapping, legs pumping like a cartoon blur. The kids flung the door open and she launched inside; dog successfully captured.

That became the ritual. Daily. Nonnegotiable.

Despite everything, the digging, the chaos, the disappearing acts, she always came running back.

That trip was hard, emotionally and physically. But it was ours. There were fights over campfire food, games of license plate bingo, midnight pee breaks in the woods, and whispered hopes I wasn't brave enough to say out loud. And there was Scooter. Always causing trouble. Always coming home.

When we finally reached Utah, it didn't feel like the end of the road. It felt like the beginning of one. We didn't have much; but we had a van, a tent, a lot of stories, and a little black dog who refused to be left behind.

And if you're going to bring a dog on a life-changing cross-country journey, make damn sure she knows how to find her bone.

*"I didn't know where the dog buried her bone,
but I knew exactly where she buried my patience."*

A BACKHOE AND A WOMAN

When we decided to become more self-sufficient in Northern Utah, we bought a little patch of land in the ancient lake basin with the most exquisite view of the mountains in Weber County. We wanted to build our own slice of paradise. Naturally, we named it, because we name just about everything, and called it "Pair A Dice." A lucky roll, a fresh start, and a dream two women were determined to make come true. It wasn't a grand ranch, just shy of 1.5 acres, but we had big plans. Chickens, gardens, greenhouses—the works.

One day, a friend suggested we get a backhoe to help tackle our long to-do list. It was something to think about, we already had one of the smaller Kubota tractors. To have a granddaddy of tractors to tackle the big jobs wasn't a bad idea, considering how much digging and moving and hauling we were about to take on. When we came across a sturdy old Case backhoe for sale, we jumped on it. We named her "A Hoe." (We couldn't help ourselves.)

She was dependable, if a bit thirsty for hydraulic fluid, and quickly became an essential part of the team. We decided Natalie would be the official operator; coordination has never been my strong suit, more like a bull in a China shop. So I would be her ground crew and expert director. It was a match made in mini-farm heaven.

Our first major project was tearing down an old, rickety chicken house. Sounds simple, right? Just swing the bucket and boom, down it goes. But there was a twist, a delicate standpipe poking out of the ground just two inches from one of the walls. If we hit that pipe, we'd basically set off a waterworks disaster, and the only way to stop it would be shutting off water to everything. And believe me, plumbing was not a language we spoke yet.

So, Natalie had to learn to maneuver that giant machine with the precision of a jeweler. Those first few swings were more like polite nudges. But with teamwork and a few deep breaths, we got it done, pipe intact, chicken house gone, and backhoe skills officially underway.

From that day forward, A Hoe was part of nearly every project we tackled. We dug holes for baby trees, pulled out ones we didn't want, laid irrigation lines, carved out foundations for a big outbuilding and a greenhouse, and once used her to gently persuade an under-construction outbuilding back where it belonged after a fierce windstorm tried to turn it into the Leaning Tower of Pisa. One day, we used her to move a massive, rusty irrigation water filtration tank like it was a lunchbox. That machine earned her keep.

Natalie became a master behind the levers. Watching her work was like watching a concert pianist. She could dig a hole with sharp edges, level out ground so smoothly you could serve pancakes on it, and peel dirt away from a basement wall with such precision that only a quarter inch of soil remained. Meanwhile, I became fluent in our own backhoe guidance sign language, a few sharp gestures, some shouted directions, and plenty of laughing.

We became a bit of a roadside attraction. Neighbors and passersby would stop to watch us work, curious to see two women and a backhoe in perfect rhythm. One day, a man paused and asked, "Can she really drive that thing?" With a deadpan face, I said, "Yes, she's driving it right now." He blinked like he'd just seen a baby chicken tap dance.

Owning A Hoe taught us more than just how to operate heavy machinery. It taught us patience, trust, communication—and the joy of tackling something completely new. With a little practice and a lot of persistence, even the most intimidating machine can become a tool for joy.

And if you're lucky, you'll find that digging into the dirt together, can bring you closer to the life you've always wanted.

Campfire and Marshmallows

Living in Northern Utah, one of the things you simply must do is go camping under the stars, preferably in one of those mountain campsites tucked beside a babbling stream. The scent of pine hangs in the cool air, and the water murmurs like it's telling secrets. Ideally, you pick a night that's not too chilly, just crisp enough to keep the mosquitoes honest.

And where there's camping, there's a campfire.

The sacred ritual: friends, family, and fellow campers gathered around. Someone might be strumming a guitar while the group sang a few old favorites like "Kumbaya" and worked on building the perfect s'more over the campfire.

You know the drill: graham crackers, a square of chocolate, and a marshmallow roasted to perfection. Now, my idea of perfection? Golden brown on all sides, soft and gooey all the way through. Not a speck of black.

Well, on this particular night, I was in my storytelling glory, doing what I do best, while gently roasting my marshmallow over the flames. Everything was going great… until that little sucker suddenly burst into flames.

I gasped.

"NOOOOO!"

For one wild second, time stopped. My precious marshmallow! I couldn't just let it go, it was nearly perfect, golden and gooey. So I did what any panicked dessert lover would do: I whipped the stick toward my face to blow it out. But the marshmallow was so soft, the flick sent it flying and launched that little fireball straight at my own face. It hit my chin and stuck.

There I was, with a little blob of fire dancing on my face, slapping wildly at my chin like I was trying to kill a very determined mosquito. I managed to put it out, but not before leaving myself a fine, blistering souvenir.

The crowd around the fire looked horrified.

"Are you okay?" they asked, wide-eyed. And in true motherly fashion, I brushed it off.

"Oh, that? Pfft. I'm fine."

Of course, I sat there the rest of the night with my chin throbbing like a tiny drum.

Two days later, when the scab bloomed into what looked like a bad lipstick experiment gone wrong, my daughter Natalie, who had witnessed the whole flaming fiasco, snapped a photo for posterity. I'm pretty sure she shared it with half the country, too.

Now, every time I smell toasted marshmallows, I can't help but smile. I may have lost a little skin that night, but I gained something better: *the legend of The Flaming Chin.*

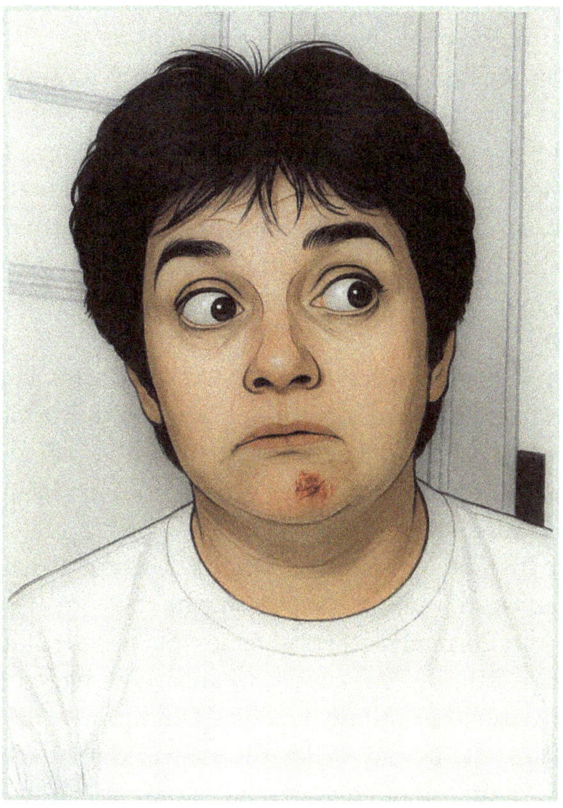

"Evidence of the night my marshmallow aimed for my chin — and won."

WHAT'S IN A NAME?

Let's talk about last names. Some folks have names that are fun, unique, or downright challenging; names that can spark interest, mischief, or sometimes just a good laugh. It all depends on how you decide to handle it. Me? I've always chosen to have fun with mine.

Now, my last name, Nigro (pronounced "Nee-grow" in Italian, rolling the R), has been the source of some entertaining moments over the years. Sure, the meaning or interpretation might shift depending on where you are, but one thing never changes: I'll find a way to turn it into a good story.

Natalie, my daughter, and I got used to hearing the same reactions, confused looks, uncertain pauses, even the occasional "Are you *sure* that's how it's spelled?" She learned early on that if someone needed to write it down, she'd better spell it right away. No hesitation, no pause for awkward guesses. That's my girl, efficient, polite, and entirely unfazed.

Back in college, we even went to the same school and occasionally found ourselves in the same class. Now, to me, it felt like an opportunity for mischief. To Natalie, it was a test in patience. We made quite the pair, one ready to rescue people from embarrassment, and one ready to cause a little fun for sport.

On the first day of one particular class, the professor was taking roll call. This wasn't just any professor, he took great pride in pronouncing names correctly, especially ones that were trickier due to cultural origins. Asian, Indian, Arabic, Spanish—he nailed them all. He would always ask after calling a name, "Did I pronounce that right?" even when he knew he did. When the answer came back with, "That is correct, sir," he'd puff out his chest like a rooster in a hen house. With each correct pronunciation, his chest grew larger. I waited with anticipation, he had reached the K's, he was getting closer. Then he came to the N's "Natalie…" he paused. You could see him wrestling with it. But Natalie was used to this and calmly said, "That's Nigro, sir. With the 'i' pronounced like 'eye."

The professor nodded, relieved. Next name on the roster? Me.

"Shirley," (I went by my real name then) he called, then hesitated. He squinted at the paper like it might bite him. I could see his wheels turning. And I just sat there, waiting for him to figure it out, tapping my fingers lightly on the desk.

Finally, with a question mark hanging in the air, he said, "Nigro?" I couldn't resist. "No, sir," I replied in a loud, clear voice and a straight face. "That's *Negro,* sir." (The proper Italian pronunciation.) Oh, the look on his face. Poor guy.

After that first day, roll call wasn't required anymore. Coincidence? I think not. But the fun didn't stop there.

About halfway through the quarter, the professor paused mid-lecture. He was in the middle of some riveting explanation when he suddenly stopped, pointed at Natalie and me—perpetual front-row sitters—and asked, "Are you two related?"

Natalie was speechless and I smiled and replied, "No, sir. We were just as surprised as you to find out we had the same last name when we sat down next to each other."

He stared at us for a moment, trying to decide if I was pulling his leg. Then he just nodded, still uncertain, and went back to lecturing. To this day, I don't know if he ever figured out the truth. Was it nice of me? Maybe not. Do I feel bad? Not one bit. Some names are too much fun to pass up.

"Two Nigros walk into a classroom…
the professor never stood a chance."

DO RE MI

One summer, back when I was living in Beaufort, South Carolina, my best friend and I got it into our heads that we were going to give our kids a summer to remember.

Between us, we had four kids, my three and her son, and plenty of enthusiasm, if not always an abundance of common sense.

We decided we'd explore all the sights around Beaufort and beyond. The smell of salt and marsh grass hung in the air, and the cicadas sang backup to our plans. Don't ask me why, but somewhere in the middle of our grand planning, we got inspired by The Sound of Music. Naturally, we figured our little traveling circus needed matching outfits. Just like the Von Trapps. Because nothing says "summer fun" like matching polyester in ninety-degree Carolina heat.

Now, finding identical outfits for two grown women and four wiggly kids, ranging from "tiny tornado" to "growing too fast for their own good," turned out to be a challenge. Shoes too! But thanks to sheer stubbornness, a clearance sale or two, and our unstoppable sense of mission, we made it happen.

Did they fit perfectly? Not really. Did they match? Sort of, if you squinted. Did we look like some wandering act that might get reported to child services? Possibly. But we were committed.

Naturally, once we had our uniforms, we needed a theme song. Obviously, we picked "Do Re Mi." We weren't exactly the Trapp Family Singers, but if you listened close, and I do mean *real* close, you could figure out what song we were trying to sing.

We even bought a couple of whistles, just in case one of our "team members" wandered off during sightseeing. Which was likely. Very likely.

The big debut for our little act was a day trip to Savannah, Georgia, about 42 miles away in my trusty old VW bus. Piece of cake.

Honestly? It went better than we expected. The bus rattled and hummed down Highway 17, every window rolled open, hair flying, voices lifting into the thick summer air. Let's just say subtlety wasn't our strong suit. But it wasn't until we spilled out in downtown Savannah that people really started to notice—the full glory of our matching outfits and questionable harmonies was impossible to miss.

People were definitely curious. Some stopped to ask who we were. A surprising number thought we were some kind of sports team.

I'm not sure which sport involves sloppy uniforms, off-key singing, and whistles used mostly for locating lost children.

We didn't get tips or any awards, but we did collect plenty of chuckles and smiles, a whole lot of curious looks, and enough stories to fill an album.

That summer was a blast—even if we never quite figured out what "team" we were pretending to be.

And looking back at the photos now? I mostly just sit there, shaking my head, thinking: "I can't believe how young I was—and how willing I was to walk around Savannah dressed like a bright red-and-yellow striped bumblebee with a whistle around my neck."

"Who needs the Von Trapps when you've got determination, clearance sales, and kids who will wear whatever you hand them?"

PARADE OF KITCHENS

Years ago, in York, PA, there was an event unlike anything I'd ever seen: The Kitchen Chef Parade of Homes.

The idea was simple but brilliant. A handful of beautiful homes opened their doors to the public, each one boasting a gourmet kitchen. And stationed in those sparkling kitchens? Professional chefs from some of the best local restaurants, cooked live, and handed out samples of their finest dishes.

Now, when I say *gourmet kitchens,* I don't mean your average countertop and a shiny toaster. These were the kind of kitchens you see on fancy cooking shows.

Somehow, Natalie and I were invited to participate. Let's be very clear, we were not chefs. Not even on our best days. But in the late 1990s, we'd written a book on healthy vegan eating called *Companion Guide to Healthy Cooking: A Practical Introduction to Natural Ingredients* (published in September 1996, for those keeping score).

It wasn't exactly a bestseller, but it had heart and a lot of great information. Thanks to that book, we'd spent a few years teaching classes all over the region—helping folks learn how to store, prep, and cook natural foods. Somehow, that was enough to land us an invite to stand in a stranger's designer kitchen and hand out healthy-based samples to the public. We said yes.

After plenty of back-and-forth, we landed on our dish: Mock Egg Salad Sandwiches. The "egg" part was tofu, mashed and seasoned just right, while everything else followed the familiar egg-salad playbook. Why tofu? Because back then, tofu was the poster child of the health food world. And we figured the familiar egg salad approach might make it a little less scary for folks who weren't quite ready to jump headfirst into vegan eating. We wanted something approachable, something that raised eyebrows in a good way.

We partnered with a generous local baker who had supported our classes in the past. He came through again, supplying us with loaf after loaf of beautiful whole wheat bread. It felt like we made hundreds of sandwiches.

On the big day, we set up in a stunning kitchen—the kind of place that made you want to cook, even if you didn't know how. The marble gleamed, the copper pots glowed, and the air already smelled faintly of something wonderful about to happen.

When the opening time arrived, people were lined up with anticipation, eager for what they were about to see, taste, and learn.

We were ready to serve and educate. Every few minutes, we gave a quick, tight three-minute talk on tofu—its uses, its benefits, and its surprisingly eggy impersonation skills. Somehow, each one came out sounding fresh, playful, and a little improvised, as if we'd just thought of it on the spot. Then we handed out sandwiches, answered questions, and did it all again. And again. And again. And again. For hours.

We probably could've won awards for consistency.

To our surprise and delight, people didn't just nibble politely, they devoured those sandwiches with gusto. When we finally revealed there wasn't a single egg in the mix, jaws dropped and eyebrows shot up. You could practically hear the collective, "Wait… this is tofu?" What started as a tofu sales pitch turned into something better: curiosity, laughter, and a few new friends who learned that tofu wasn't quite the scary mystery they'd imagined. And the best part? That mock egg salad didn't just pass the taste test. It showed up, showed off, and took a bow.

"Turns out, sometimes you don't need to be a five-star chef to make a five-star memory."

"Tofu pretending to be eggs, us pretending to be chefs."

From Pearls to Plaid

Once upon a time, back in the late 60s and 70s, I was an Officer's Wife in the Naval Civil Engineer's Corps. That title came with a uniform, even if it was never officially issued. Dress codes were not suggestions. They were law, gospel, etiquette, and a competitive sport disguised as good manners.

Luncheons, Hail and Farewells, VIP dinners, and three full-blown Balls every year all demanded perfection. I delivered. Pearls, long gloves, three-inch heels, and dresses that required careful breathing. My hair was sprayed into submission, my lipstick stayed put through cocktails and polite smiles, and I could look delighted while my feet quietly plotted revenge.

Picture me walking into a room lined with Commanding Officers' wives, each one scanning me from hairline to hem with the efficiency of airport security. Did your clutch match your shoes? Were your gloves appropriate for the season? Was your posture saying "poised" or "new girl who missed a memo"?

Some events were elaborate multi-course dinners with linen tablecloths and napkins thick enough to upholster a chair. This was not a grab-a-burger situation. There were forks for reasons nobody explained, and glasses that appeared mid-meal like magic. I learned quickly that choosing the wrong utensil could doom you faster than spilling wine. I could select the correct fork every time and introduce a Rear Admiral without breaking a sweat. It was not elegance. It was training.

Every gathering came with unspoken rules. Dresses long and modest, never flashy. Hair neat. Voice soft. Smile permanent. You were part hostess, part diplomat, and part unpaid brand ambassador for your husband's career. You learned to nod thoughtfully, laugh politely, and keep certain opinions locked up tight.

If you were ever unsure what the dress code was for an event, all you had to do was check with the commanding officer's wife. She would explain, in loving detail, exactly what was expected. Hem length, glove length, heel height. It was delivered kindly, but make no mistake, compliance was assumed.

I got very good at this role. Too good. I could dress for any occasion, hold pleasant conversation with anyone, and make discomfort look elegant. From the outside, it all sparkled. From the inside, it felt like wearing a corset you could never unlatch.

Eventually, the marriage ended, and with it went my career as a military wife. The day I tossed most of my wardrobe and my last pair of pantyhose was not sad. It was glorious. It felt like stepping out of a costume and into oxygen. Fewer rules, less ceremony, and a whole lot less smiling on command.

These days, my dress code is brutally simple. Is it clean, or at least clean enough. And can I sit, stand, and live my life without suffering.

Fashion choices? Simplified.

If I like a shirt, I buy five. Done. I still have a uniform, but this one is mine. Plaid flannel, soft jeans, and shoes that do not require painkillers. Comfort is king.

Do not mistake it for giving up. This is freedom. This is wisdom earned from years of matching handbags to gloves. This is me living out loud, soft, cozy, and just a smidge rebellious.

And if I show up wearing the same shirt five days in a row?

That is not laziness. That is branding.

"I can still clean up nice — I just don't have to anymore."

When the Walls were Paper

Now, back in 1969, our little crew got planted in Yokosuka, Japan. The Navy dropped us there with a cheerful "good luck" and no base housing to be found. So, we nabbed ourselves a lovely little place out in the economy. It sounds fancy but really just means we had to learn how to say "rent" and "does this come with heat?" in Japanese.

It was a traditional Japanese home, the kind with tatami mats that smell like sun-warmed straw and sliding doors made of wood and rice paper. Peaceful. Simple. Very different.

Now, Miss Natalie had just figured out how to walk, and more importantly, how to reach things. And oh, those paper doors were just her height. Soft, mysterious, and oh-so-satisfying when poked by chubby fingers still slick from thumb-sucking.

One day, she pressed her damp little hand against the paper, and poof! Just like magic, the paper dissolved under her fingers like cotton candy in a summer rain. Her eyes lit up like she'd discovered the holy grail of sensory experiences.

After that, it became a full-time job for her. You could measure her growth by the missing paper on the door. I'm telling you, that girl had the precision of a beaver with a tape measure.

By the time summer rolled in, there wasn't a scrap of paper left below the three-foot mark. Not a single square inch survived her curious little touch. Eventually, we gave up trying to tape it or patch it. We leaned into the chaos, took the rest down, and turned the house into a breezy, paperless wonderland.

But winter came, as it does, and so did our kind landlady—with fresh paper and a look that said, "You Americans are... enthusiastic." She patiently repapered every door, and by then Natalie had moved on to other mysteries, like how to wear a tea towel like a ballgown and sing to birds.

Turns out, those paper panels weren't just for show. They were the poor man's insulation. And maybe a quiet parenting tool too. They taught Natalie that actions have soggy little consequences. And they taught me that sometimes, it's better to laugh than to scream into a tatami mat.

Looking back, I must admit, that old house taught us a lot more than just how to say "rent" in Japanese. It taught me to loosen up, to find the humor when things didn't go quite as planned, and to appreciate the patience of kind strangers who quietly repapered doors without a word of complaint.

Years later, whenever I see a sliding paper door in a movie or travel show, I can still hear the soft little pop Natalie's tiny fingers made as they broke through the paper — like bubble wrap for toddlers. We left a few giggles (and a lot of replacement paper) behind in Yokosuka, but I carried the memories home, and they've never worn thin.

"Natalie's home improvement phase: 100% demo, 0% repairs."

FINANCIAL SHOCK THERAPY

Raising three teenagers on a tight budget was never easy, but I had a philosophy: *if you're old enough to make a baby, you're old enough to manage a budget.* It was time for some Trouble-style economics. I wasn't raising freeloaders: I was raising future adults who could face the world with a wallet and some wisdom.

Now, we were considered poor, but my kids still acted like I was some kind of ATM with a limitless balance. Back then, long-distance phone calls cost money. Friends in another city? Dollars down the drain. Designer clothes? Out of reach. And don't even get me started on "only the best" music lessons so someone could earn first chair in the high school jazz band.

At that point, I was divorced and living on Navy child support. Their father and I had agreed: support until each kid turned eighteen, and then they were on their own. Which meant it was time to teach them what that actually felt like before they got thrown into the deep end!

So, one evening I gathered the troops at the kitchen table and said, "Okay, listen up. Each of you is getting one-third of the child support. It'll go straight into your own bank account at the start of each month."

You'd have thought I'd just announced they'd won the lottery. They cheered. They hugged. They looked like someone had just given them superpowers.

Then I smiled sweetly and said, "But… there's a catch."

And that's when they froze.

Now, these weren't just any kids. These were *my* kids — veterans of Trouble's "life lesson" ambushes. They knew that when I said "catch," it never meant something normal like taking out the trash. No, my catches came wrapped in life skills, character-building, and usually a little chaos. So, three pairs of eyes locked on me, wide with that mix of suspicion and surrender that said, Oh no… what's she up to this time?"

"You'll each pay a fourth of the household bills: rent, water, electricity, phone, the whole shebang. You'll also buy your own food, clothes, and back-to-school stuff. I'll cover doctor visits and braces. The rest? Yours to spend or save. But when it's gone, it's gone."

The silence that followed was almost holy.

Now, you have to understand. This wasn't your run-of-the-mill allowance operation. I had a great relationship with our local bank manager, and she *loved* the idea. She set up three personal checking accounts and practically turned the tellers into financial coaches. Every month, those sweet ladies would cheer the kids on, ask about their saving goals, and occasionally raise an eyebrow when a balance ran low. It was small-town economics at its finest.

When the first round of bills hit, we sat down again. Me with my stack of envelopes and them with their shiny new checkbooks. "All right, team," I said, "time to pay the bills."

Gasps all around. "You mean we have to pay for garbage pickup?!" one asked. "Yes, darling," I said, "the city doesn't come out of the goodness of its heart."

When they realized how little was left for luxuries, the looks on their faces could've won Best Dramatic Performance at the 'The Day Reality Hit' Awards.

Month two rolled around, and one of the kids didn't have his share. Oh, the drama that followed. Since our deal meant we (meaning the three of us who did have our money in order) had to make up the difference, the other two glared at their sibling with the righteous fury of people who'd done everything right and were now paying for someone else's mistake. I decided not to ask what happened behind closed doors, but let's just say the other two *handled it*. Whatever went down, the message stuck. That "can't pay my part" problem never happened again.

Then came the real fun.

Before this experiment, when I'd buy one kid a new shirt, the other two would immediately demand one too. But once the money came from *their* accounts? Poof! That "me-too" entitlement disappeared overnight. They spent differently, proudly, and sometimes foolishly—but they owned every decision.

One bought fancy clothes and left them in a pile on the floor like art. Another hoarded books until her shelf looked like a miniature library. The third skipped pricey music lessons altogether, still earned first chair in the band, and eventually paid his own way to Germany for the summer.

Each thought the other two were spending like lunatics, but they respected the independence. And that was the real magic.

Soon, they each wanted more cash flow. So, they got creative: paper routes, mowing lawns, helping me in my dog grooming business. If they wanted a car, they had to buy it themselves—and pay for their own insurance, too. (Which, let's be honest, was *way* worse for the boys.) Every one of them eventually bought their own "vehicle." And by that, I mean four-wheeled death traps that would make today's parents faint. But hey, it was freedom.

Then came my favorite experiment: credit cards. I convinced the bank to give each of them a card with a $300 limit. Secretly, I guaranteed them. I wanted the kids to learn about interest, temptation, and that magical lie called "minimum payment."

And learn they did. Those balances maxed out faster than a sailor on payday.

Being good little customers who paid on time, the bank started raising their limits—$500, then $1,000, then $1,500. The kids thought they were winning. The bank thought it had fresh bait.

Then their father found out. Oh, he was horrified. "Irresponsible!" he said, and promptly paid off all their balances to "teach them a lesson they wouldn't forget."

The lesson they learned? Free money!

Within a few months, every single one of them was right back to a $1,500 limit.

Eventually, reality caught up. Those payments started to sting. Slowly but surely, they clawed their way back down to zero. And discovered something priceless: freedom feels better than shopping.

These days, they've got mortgages and responsibilities, but they carry zero credit card debt. They know how to budget, save, and pay what's due. And they can sniff out a bad deal faster than you can say "introductory rate."

Life teaches lessons.

But moms? We teach with love, laughter, and the occasional real-life line item.

And if I'm honest, seeing my kids financially steady, smart about money, and confident in their choices? That's the kind of return on investment no bank can match.

"And this, children, is why Mom drinks… wine. Lots of wine. No children were harmed in the making of this budget (emotionally… maybe)."

Sandstone, Shutter Clicks, and Shenanigans

When I went back to college in my late thirties, I had a brilliant idea: I'd major in psychology. It made sense. I was curious about people, endlessly fascinated by why we do the things we do, and already had plenty of life experience to draw from.

What I didn't realize at first was that a bachelor's degree in psychology didn't actually require all that many psychology classes. To graduate, I needed a certain number of total credit hours, which meant I had to pad my schedule with electives. And once I decided I wasn't planning to apply to graduate school, those electives didn't need to impress an admissions committee. They just needed to keep me interested.

I already knew my way around a camera, so choosing photography classes was the perfect blend of practical and pleasurable. They were "easy" credits in the best possible way, and they gave me the freedom to dig deeper into something I genuinely loved.

One course caught my attention: a three-day photography adventure in Southern Utah, one big credit, and open to anyone with no strings attached. It sounded too good to be true, but I signed up anyway and convinced my daughter and roommate, Natalie, to come along. (After all, I couldn't risk being the "old person" surrounded by a herd of 20-something college kids. Natalie = safety net.)

And let me tell you, it was fantastic.

We packed up multiple vans with students, cameras, and enough snacks and booze to fuel a road trip apocalypse. The rules were simple: if someone yelled "STOP!" the whole caravan screeched to a halt while we all tumbled out, cameras blazing, racing to capture the perfect shot.

Picture it: twenty or more young adults sprinting across the desert, camera bags bouncing at their sides, lenses flashing in the desert sun, and laughter echoing off red canyon walls. The air smelled like sage, dust, and pure freedom.

We made up ridiculous stories to entertain curious onlookers. "Oh yes, we're part of a top-secret National Geographic assignment," we'd joke. The result? A weekend full of laughter, incredible memories, good food and booze and some impressive photos.

The kids didn't mind an "old fart" joining their fun; I just fit in. I was simply another slightly offbeat, camera-toting dreamer chasing the perfect shot.

Fast forward a few decades (don't ask how many). I decided to give those photos a modern twist, editing, stylizing, and framing them to hang proudly on my bedroom wall. Each one carries the color of the Utah desert and the memory of a moment when I said yes to something just because it sounded fun.

Voilà! These pieces aren't just photos. They're little slices of 1989, each one reminding me that Southern Utah's beauty, spontaneity, warmth, and laughter never age. They're proof that adventure doesn't come with an age limit.

So here they are, my *Artwork of Utah's Past*.

"Instead of sitting in a classroom, I chased sunsets and sandstone. These photos were my assignments, my art projects, and my little excuse to get out and explore. Southern Utah gave me an A — and a whole lot of beautiful memories."

THE SCANNER HATES ME

I want it on the record: I love tools. Truly, I do. They're marvels of engineering that make life easier and work more productive. But every now and then, one of those tools decides to stage a mutiny. And let me tell you, nothing has ever rebelled against me like the large-format scanner.

In our architectural drawing proofreading business, we'd check commercial building plans for errors—marking them up with a rainbow of colors and a lot of bright, accusatory red. Once we were done, and before shipping the drawings back to the design team, we'd scan every single one of them. Why? So that if the shipping gods got creative with their chaos, we'd still have a record of our hard, time-consuming, and much-needed work.

Now, when I say "drawings," I don't mean a couple of sheets. I'm talking hundreds—sometimes thousands—of oversized pages, each one roughly the size of a picnic blanket. Guess who got assigned to operate the scanner. That's right: low person on the totem pole, me.

Scanning was tedious at best, but when the scanner jammed, it became a nightmare. Clearing the jam, restarting the machine, and renaming files to keep them in order all took time, far too much of it. And if a document wrinkled in the process? Well, that was a special kind of torment, trying to smooth it out and run it through again with nothing but hope, prayer, and crossed fingers.

Needless to say, I developed a... colorful vocabulary during this process. One particularly offensive word became my go-to whenever the scanner acted up. Eventually, I started calling the machine by that word exclusively. Let's just say the name wasn't very nice. If you put "BASS" and "TURD" together, that was the scanner's name.

One day, after I unleashed a particularly loud tirade, Natalie appeared. "You know," she said in her maddeningly calm voice, "if you keep calling the scanner something negative, it might just respond negatively. Maybe, if you gave it a positive name, it would behave better."

I stared at her, my mouth half-open, ready to argue, but then stopped. She did have a point. I had nothing to lose, so I changed the name to Pal. From that moment on, it wasn't my enemy anymore.

And would you believe it? Things improved.

Sure, the scanner still jammed now and then—it wasn't a miracle worker—but I didn't feel quite so murderous about it. I'd just sigh, clear the jam, and say, "Come on, Pal, let's try this again." Somehow, naming it something friendly softened the experience.

By the time we finished scanning those thousands of drawings, Pal and I had developed an understanding. I didn't curse at it, and it didn't eat the drawings. Much.

So, the moral of the story? Sometimes, a little rebranding goes a long way. And in the end, Pal taught me one surprising truth: sometimes what needs fixing isn't the machine—it's the attitude of the operator. Even if it's just for your sanity.

"A little name change turned a paper-chewing monster into my Pal. Some battles are best solved with kindness — and a few deep sighs."

TODAY, I GOT MY "FLIPPER!"

What's a Flipper, you ask? No, it's not a dolphin. It's a removable set of fake teeth. The kind you never imagine owning until life taps you on the shoulder and says, "Surprise."

A few years ago, I had a nasty jaw infection that took out three of my teeth. Just like that. Gone. No dramatic farewell, no final meal. One day they were mine, the next day they were a dental memory.

Naturally, I asked my dentist what could be done. He shrugged and said, "We could do a partial, but they don't always stay in very well. And with how much you talk, you might spit it out mid-sentence."

Mid-sentence.

That was all I needed to hear. I had no interest in punctuating my conversations by launching dental hardware across the room. I decided missing teeth were far less embarrassing than *traveling* teeth.

And honestly, I adjusted just fine. I learned how to chew like a professional. I avoided biting into apples unless they were sliced, peeled, and nonjudgmental. I could still take down a steak, and I convinced myself my smile had character. A little rough around the edges, sure, but so am I. I even leaned into it. Toothless redneck charm. Own it or it owns you.

Then I moved to St. George and met my new dentist. Smooth. Confident. The kind of man who smiles like he knows things about you before you say a word. He looked in my mouth and casually asked if I'd ever considered a Flipper.

I told him the truth. I didn't think I needed one. I was eating just fine, thank you very much. These remaining choppers of mine can still tear into a steak like a champ. Besides, at my age, I wasn't exactly trying to win any beauty contests.

But this dentist had a way with words. He didn't pressure me, didn't lecture, didn't scare me with charts or diagrams. He just smiled and said, "You might be surprised how much you like it."

I should have recognized manipulation when I heard it.

So this morning, I got fitted. And let me tell you, nothing reminds you of your age quite like someone snapping fake teeth into your mouth and telling you to "try talking now."

I sounded ridiculous. I lisped. I whistled. Certain words came out wrong enough to qualify as a foreign language. Natalie laughed so hard she had to grab the counter, which did wonders for my confidence.

But the real adventure came later.

Nobody tells you that taking a Flipper out is not a simple process. You don't just remove it. You coax it. You negotiate. You gently pry while hoping you don't pull something loose that was never meant to move. The first few times, I was convinced I might need pliers, a mirror, and a calm adult in the room.

Eventually, I figured it out.

Turns out, wearing a Flipper is an art form. Like learning a secret handshake with your own mouth. Awkward, slightly humiliating, but strangely empowering once you get the hang of it.

I'm still practicing. But now, when I smile, all my teeth show up for duty.

At this stage of my life, I didn't expect to be learning new tricks, especially ones involving removable body parts. Yet here I am.

Still adapting. Still laughing. Still getting fitted for the next version of myself.

"Fancy new teeth, same old big mouth."

What Happened to My Nickel?

When I was a curious and gullible five-year-old, my big sister, three and a half years older than me, had one favorite pastime: teasing me.

One day, she announced that she could do magic. "Show me!" I begged, eyes wide with excitement. She wouldn't consent right away and made me beg for quite a while first.

But then, with the flair of a seasoned magician, she pulled out a dime, popped it into her mouth, and then announced she'd swallowed it. For proof, she opened her mouth—no dime in sight. Then, with dramatic precision she placed her hand on her stomach, moved it very slowly upward, and, ta-da! The dime popped back out of her mouth. Magic. I was completely in awe.

A couple of days later, I received my usual allowance: a shiny nickel. I was bursting with excitement to try the "magic trick" my sister had shown me. So, naturally, I swallowed the nickel. Then I placed my hand on my stomach, just like she demonstrated, and slowly moved it upward. I opened my mouth dramatically, expecting the nickel to appear like... magic.

But nothing happened. I tried again. And again. Still nothing. Panic set in. I rushed to my sister and confessed, "I swallowed my nickel! You have to get it back!" Her face went pale. "You WHAT?!" she shrieked.

When I explained, she called me stupid and admitted that she hadn't really swallowed her dime. It was just hidden under her tongue. There was no magic, just a trick.

Now we were both panicking. Did swallowing a nickel mean certain death? Would I survive? We had no choice but to tell our parents, a prospect almost scarier than swallowing the coin itself.

My parents did not find the situation amusing. My dad muttered something about "natural consequences," and their grand solution? My sister was put on "nickel patrol," which meant examining my waste for the next four days to confirm the nickel had passed. To say she was less than thrilled with this task would be an under-statement. I personally felt she might have been more motivated to do a thorough job if the patrol continued until the nickel was actually found, but apparently after four days, the mystery was declared "close enough."

Despite her semi-diligent monitoring, the nickel didn't appear. Either she missed it, or it was still lurking somewhere inside me. Several more days passed with no sign of my lost fortune. Then, one morning during my usual potty time, I glanced into the toilet and spotted something.

A penny. My heart skipped a beat. Where did that come from?

But a penny is a penny. I was hoping for my nickel, but I wasn't about to let it go to waste. I fished it out (don't judge—I was five), washed it off thoroughly, and marveled at my "treasure." As the water rinsed away the grime, my penny transformed... back into my swallowed nickel.

Eureka!

I was overjoyed to have my allowance back, even if it took a week to resurface. I'll refrain from commenting on the cleanliness of money in general, and yes, I proudly spent it on a movie, none the worse for wear.

Lesson learned: leave the "magic tricks" to my sister—she's full of tricks but fresh out of magic.

"The day I learned two things: sisters lie, and plumbing works."

A Lesson on the Rocks

When my kids were teenagers, we had a lot of "talk time" moments. Some were heartfelt, some were ridiculous, and some lived in that gray area where you're not sure which category they belong in until years later. Parenting teenagers is like that. You show up with good intentions and hope nobody brings it up in therapy later.

One of those conversations kicked off when one of their friends announced, with great pride, that he drank Screwdrivers because he couldn't taste the alcohol. He said it like he'd cracked some kind of life code. Bonus points, apparently, if you could drink without noticing what you were doing.

That comment flipped on my internal "teachable moment" radar, which, for better or worse, has a hair trigger.

I said, "Look, alcohol is food. It's meant to be enjoyed, like anything else you put in your body. If your goal is to escape the world, there are easier ways. Take up photography. Go skiing. Try skydiving. Or heck, become a workaholic, a clean-a-holic, or a golf-a-holic. At least those won't erase your brain cells while you're at it."

They listened. Sort of. Teenagers are excellent at listening with their eyes while their minds wander off to something much more interesting. That's when the idea hit me.

What followed was a week-long Taste Test Experiment. Strictly educational, of course. For science. We went to the liquor store and bought mini bottles of whiskey, scotch, vodka, and gin. We covered the full range, from bottom-shelf swill to top-shelf treasures. If we were going to do this, we were going to do it properly, which is how most of my parenting philosophies have gone slightly sideways over the years.

Each night, we'd sample a few and compare notes like the world's most underqualified beverage connoisseurs. No chugging, no bravado. Just small sips, thoughtful pauses, and commentary that swung wildly between profound and completely uninformed.

The reactions were priceless.

One kid declared that the cheap gin tasted like gasoline. Without thinking, I asked how he knew what gasoline tasted like. The look on his face answered the question, and I decided that was a road best left unexplored.

We talked about smell, burn, aftertaste. About how some drinks hit sharp and angry, while others eased in like they belonged there. Each night, we set the winning empty mini bottle aside, price tag and all, so no one could argue later about which one had earned top honors. I wasn't about to rely on teenage memory for something this important. That way lay chaos. And repeat experiments. Neither of which appealed to me.

By the end of the week, the lesson was clear. Cheap booze is awful. Truly awful. The good stuff, though, was worth savoring. Not gulping. Not hiding behind juice. Just appreciating what it was.

Fast-forward to today.

If my kids drink, they drink the good stuff. But more than that, they respect it. They know what's in the glass, where it came from, and how it's supposed to taste. They tease me and say it's my fault they can't drink anything cheap anymore, and I take that as a compliment.

Now, whenever I visit, I know that whatever drink they hand me will be top-drawer. A small, satisfying proof that some lessons really do age well.

Cheers to life lessons that stick.

*"Some lessons go down smoother than others.
Proof that parenting sometimes requires… proof."*

3 Big Pigs

When I lived out in the country near Beaufort, SC, I had what you might call an interesting neighbor. No, not a person, a pig farm. And occasionally, the pigs decided to take a little vacation from their pen and come visit me.

Now, let me set the scene: These weren't the cute, pink piglets you see in cartoons. These pigs were enormous, with an attitude to match their size. They'd stare you down like, "What are you gonna do about it?" And when a pig that weighs as much as a small car looks at you that way, you start to question your life choices.

I had three young kids at the time, and they were understandably terrified of these unexpected visitors. And wouldn't you know it, there were three pigs, a big macho male and two females. I swear that male pig thought he was some kind of knight in shining armor, ready to defend his ladies. Every time they showed up, I had to call the farmer to come get them. Apparently, they preferred my place. Maybe they liked the décor?

One day, we were all out working on an old three-horse stable, fixing it up to turn into a woodshop. Everything was going fine until, you guessed it, the pigs arrived. They waddled right up and decided to pin us inside.

We were safe inside, but those pigs had made themselves right at home. That big male stood there, glaring at me with that same "What are you gonna do?" look. Well, I wasn't about to be outsmarted or cowed by a pig.

By pure luck, I had a BB gun with me. Now, don't get me wrong, this was not some high-powered weapon. It was one of those wimpy BB guns that wouldn't even dent a soda can. But I had an idea.

I figured if I could give that big male pig a little sting, he might decide it was time to go home. I didn't want to hurt him and I'm not sure I even could, *they were practically bulletproof with all that fat,* but I needed him to go home. So, I took aim… and I went for the most sensitive target I could think of.

That's right. I aimed for the male pig's, uh… family jewels.

I hit the target dead-on. He let out a little grunt, gave me a look of pure indignation, and then decided he'd had enough of my hospitality. He turned tail and ran straight home, and his two girlfriends followed right after him.

And you know what? They never came back. Guess I solved my pig problem that day, one BB at a time.

Never underestimate a mama with a BB gun and a plan.

"Never bring an attitude to a BB gun fight."

THE NIGHT I ATTACKED THE CAPTAIN

Once upon a time, I was a Naval Officer's wife. Back then, there were certain events you were expected to attend, like the monthly "Hail and Farewell" celebrations for incoming and outgoing officers. It was a semiformal affair, which meant cocktail dresses for the ladies and those crisp white dress uniforms for the gentlemen.

These evenings always included a buffet filled with fancy little bites: tiny sandwiches, seafood, fried treats, desserts, and mystery foods galore. It was supposed to double as dinner, so naturally, everyone piled their plates high with whatever looked appetizing (or at least edible).

One night, I was chatting with the commanding officer of the base and his wife, plate in hand. I was deep in conversation, nodding, smiling, listening politely, when I popped a little fried morsel into my mouth. Instantly, my body betrayed me.

My taste buds sounded the alarm before my brain even caught up: Liver. My personal culinary kryptonite. I have a sixth sense for it, a kind of superhuman liver radar. My eyes had been fooled, my attention distracted by conversation, but my tongue. Oh, it knew.

My immediate reaction? Spit it out. And I did, without grace, without warning, and with far more velocity than you'd expect from a bite-sized horror.

Unfortunately, that greasy little villain didn't drop politely onto my plate. No, it launched itself across the air like a torpedo and landed squarely on the captain's pristine white uniform, right above his ribbon bars.

His wife let out a tiny, high-pitched gasp that echoed through the room like a sonar ping. Every head turned. The captain looked down at his chest, then up at me, blinking.

Needless to say, it wasn't a career-advancing moment.

I offered a napkin and a deeply mortified apology, while mentally preparing to fake a fainting spell if needed. But to his credit, the captain just chuckled, dabbed at the stain, and said, "Well, that's one way to express your opinion."

And with that, he carried on as though being hit with airborne organ meat was part of the night's entertainment... ever the picture of composure and command.

And that is how I earned a reputation. Not for diplomacy, but for projectile honesty.

"In my defense, it looked like something else."

TOOLS, KIDS, AND A POEM

I came across some old memorabilia today, and I couldn't wait to write a story about it.

Back in 1978, I got divorced in Beaufort, South Carolina. I bought a little three bedroom house off the beaten path, just me and the kids, who were still in elementary school. Bills were due, and the bank account was light, so I got creative. I placed an ad in the local newspaper's want ads section. (And if that doesn't age me right there, bless your heart.)

I was looking for odd jobs. Fix-it work, small repairs, painting, yard work, whatever I could do. I didn't say "handywoman" because that wasn't a thing folks said back then. I just put myself out there and hoped for the best.

One day the phone rang.

The man on the other end didn't realize I was a woman, my voice has always been a little deep and smoky. Once he figured it out, he quizzed me on tools like I was interviewing for NASA. I must've passed, or maybe no one else wanted to work for him. Either way, he said, "I'll give you a try."

So, I went to work for Mr. Friedemann, a man well into his seventies with a big property and an even bigger list of home improvement projects. Job security, baby. I worked five days a week, half-days mostly, and sometimes I brought the kids along. With permission, of course. He lived by the river, and the kids thought it was heaven.

They loved him immediately. And Mr. Friedemann? He was putty in their little hands.

One day the kids came inside right before quitting time, looking like they'd crawled out of a swamp. Wet, muddy, messy little creatures. I didn't want to scold them, but I did want to make a point. So, I said, "I was thinking of taking you out for pizza, but not now, you're a mess!"

Without missing a beat, Mr. Friedemann told them, "Take off your clothes."

Before I could so much as blink, he was up from his chair, helping them peel off their muddy clothes with a laugh that filled the kitchen. He handed the bundle to his wife, called for a towel, and set to work wiping them clean... gentle as a grandpa, precise as a man who knew the value of care. There was no awkwardness, no hesitation, just pure kindness in motion.

Since it was going to take a while, he offered me a beer while we waited for the kids clothes to be laundered. I didn't say no. We played a few games, drank a little, laughed a lot.

Before we left, he pulled me aside, handed me more than enough money for pizza (and then some), and said, "My treat."

That's just who he was.

We all adored Mr. Friedemann. He became a chapter in our lives that none of us ever forgot. After several months, we decided to move to Utah. I was heartbroken to leave. Before we left, he handed the kids a few pieces of paper, he had written a poem just for them.

That poem was titled "Farewell", and let me tell you, it wasn't just a poem, it was a blessing.

It was wise and funny and heartfelt, written by a man who had lived a long time and learned how to love without any fuss. It was his way of wrapping his arms around my kids one last time. He told them to love themselves. That some love will sneak up on you like summer out of season. And that even if they forgot him, he'd tried, because new friends at threescore-and-ten were hard to come by.

Years later, my daughter Natalie, who was just a little girl when we left Beaufort, wrote a poem of her own. She was in 11th grade, and the assignment was to write about someone who meant something to her.

Her poem, "A Friend," was for Mr. Friedemann.

It's short and sweet and sincere, and it shows how much of an impression he made on her. That man wasn't just a job or a neighbor—he was a memory stitched into our family quilt.

Every once in a while, I still run into people who remind me of him — folks who fix more than they break and make the world better one little repair at a time. If Mr. Friedemann were around today, I think he'd still be out there by the river, patching up fences, writing poems, and making sure nobody leaves hungry. People like that don't fade; they just hand you a wrench and a lesson and trust you'll pass it on.

Natalie and I found both poems recently, tucked away in some old papers. Reading them brought tears to our eyes, because...

Love doesn't care about time.

WHAT COMES NEXT ARE NOT JUST POEMS

They are *keepsakes*.

They were never meant to be published. Never written for a crowd. Just a farewell from a kind old man with a soft heart and a pen... and a reply, years later, from a girl who hadn't forgotten.

Each poem tells a side of the same truth—that love leaves fingerprints.
That sometimes a goodbye becomes a gift.
And that when someone sees your muddy-kneed, pizza-loving child-self as worthy of a blessing, you remember.

So let's pause here.

Take a breath.

And step into these poems as they were given—one page at a time,
handwritten and full of heart.

PATENT AND TRADE-MARK CAUSES

Paul E. Friedemann
STAR ROUTE NO. 5 BOX 204
BEAUFORT, S. C.
29902

REGISTRY NO. 13036
AREA CODE 803-524-5034

6-6-78

This poem is dedicated to the children, Natalie, Todd & Kirk of the brilliant Shirley C. Nigro.

Dear Natalie, Todd & Kirk

Farewell

"This is no letter to the world,
– That never wrote to me."
These are some words that I have told,
To those who are leaving me.

These gems of thought, come from my heart,
But are difficult to string,
With words of art, that tell the thought,
Of a very poignant thing.

Years and years have spunn me 'round,
While yours are just begun.
May many years spinn you around.
May all your plans get done.

AND
ARK

Paul E. Friedemann
STAR ROUTE NO. 5 BOX 204
BEAUFORT, S. C.
29902

REGISTRY NO. 13036
AREA CODE 803-524-5034

I gleaned some wisdom at rare times;
Too often I gleaned none.
May you glean wisdom o'er the years;
Yet manage to have fun.

There will be those whom you should love,
And you will likely do it.
With others love comes naturally,
There's no compulsion to it.

A central one whom you should love.—
And this forsooth is true.
This love is blessed from above,
This central one is you.

And some you'll love without your leave,
And with no rhyme nor reason;
And you'll be warmed without your leave
Like summer out of season.

I bless all journies you may take,
And all your years to come,
And may you never have to stake,
Your life 'ere you go home.

I wish my blessings had the power,
That is by them implied;
But if my blessings go astray,
Remember I have tried.

III

TENT AND
ADE-MARK
CAUSES

Paul E. Friedemann
STAR ROUTE NO. 5 BOX 204
BEAUFORT, S. C.
29902

REGISTRY NO. 13036
AREA CODE 803-524-5034

An old man's blessings have great power,
So it's by folk lore stated.
His blessings do show his good will,
Beyond that they're over-rated.

And if you have some love to spare,
And don't know where to put it.
Just think of me 'cause I do care,
As long as, "I am with-it."

"How sweet if I am not forgot",
By you who're going away,
'Cause new friends at threescore-and-
ten,
Are very scarce today.

And if per chance we're for-
tunate,
To meet some years from now,
Please do not look at me and see
Just age — though that be true.
But with kind self-love look and see,
In me, your future you.

50

Natalie Nigro
A.P. Prep. Eng. 11 pd.3
10/23/84

A Friend

Some time ago, you did say
Some things that were just for me.
And now that I'm old enough to ~~comphend~~, comprehend
I see you've helped give me a key.

The gems of thought that came from you
Of a man so old and wise
Will be my guide for what is true
On the occasions that arise.

The person I should love you told,
Should be me, the central one.
You should know because you're old
And my life has just begun.

I won't forget you, my dear old friend,
Through the years that I do live
Your wisdom that you did lend
Will be a present for me to give.

"I still smile when I read his words. Even now, those simple little pages feel like a gift that's still being opened. The kids grew up. The years flew by. But Mr. Friedemann's poem? It stayed right here — a gentle reminder that sometimes, when life hands you an unexpected friend, you don't forget. You just carry them with you, wherever the years may go."

NAUGHTY ORNAMENT INCIDENT

When Christmas rolls around each year, certain memories float back like old friends. And one that always brings a grin is a story from the time Natalie and I were working at an RV park in Bernardo, New Mexico.

We had a guest at the park, a wonderfully talented woman who had the most incredible gift for working with teeny, tiny beads. She created breathtaking Christmas ornaments: delicate glass bulbs draped in intricate beadwork, every strand perfectly placed. Each one looked like it belonged in a department store window or an art gallery. And that year, she gifted several of us with her beautiful creations. We were all thrilled to receive such thoughtful, handmade treasures... well, almost everyone.

You see, one particular ornament, the one she gave to the park manager, sparked a bit of an unexpected reaction. It was stunning, no doubt. But as I looked at it, my mouth got ahead of my brain, as it's been known to do.

I blurted out: "That looks just like a whorehouse!" The entire room froze. Forks hovered midair, mouths hung open, and even the tinsel seemed to stop shimmering for a moment. Finally, someone found their voice and asked: "What?! How would YOU know what a whorehouse looks like?"

Now, I couldn't just leave them thinking I'd been guessing, or worse, that I was speaking from firsthand experience. These people knew me better than that. And judging by their grins, they were dying for the story they knew was coming. So I told them.

Years earlier, back when I was grooming dogs, I had a client who asked for something a little out of the ordinary: after finishing his dog's grooming, could I deliver the dog to his place of business? I normally didn't offer delivery service, but for some reason that day, I said yes. Big mistake.

The address he gave me was on 25th Street in Ogden, Utah. Now, if you're familiar with 25th Street today, you know it's full of charming little shops, restaurants, and historic buildings. But back then? Let's just say it hadn't quite reached its current "historic charm" status. At the time, it was still mostly pawn shops, payday loan providers, dive bars, and some... let's call them alternative businesses.

I pulled up to the address, my stomach sinking as I took in the barred windows and rundown surroundings. But I had a job to do, so I went in.

The front room seemed harmless enough, comfy furniture, a nice person at the desk, but then I was directed to carry the dog down the hall into a back room. As I walked, my suspicions grew. The carpet turned to deep red plush, the lighting dimmed, and a soft glow shimmered off satin walls.

And then I saw it. A huge open room, softly lit, with rows of double beds stretching out on both sides. Not just plain beds either, oh no. Each one was decked out with bead-and-lace canopies, deep red bedspreads, satin pillows, and the sort of atmosphere you don't often find at your typical dog owner's business.

That's when it hit me: "I'm standing in a whorehouse." I set the dog down exactly where I was told, turned on my heel, and practically sprinted out. After that, I made myself one promise: no more dog deliveries. Ever.

So, when I saw that manager's ornament, with its rich red base and elaborate beaded drapery, it triggered one very specific memory. Beautiful, yes. But let's just say it reminded me of a particular style of interior decorating I hadn't expected to stumble across. And that is how I know what a whorehouse looks like, or at least one that was ready for business and fully accessorized.

In the end, Christmas isn't just about the gifts we unwrap. It's about the stories we carry, the unexpected moments, and the memories we pass down. That ornament wasn't just a decoration, it became one more story in the big, tangled, wonderful string of lights that make up my life.

Uninvited and Unstoppable

When living in the rural outskirts of Beaufort, South Carolina, I was always on the hunt for shortcuts to make life just a smidge easier. When you've got three-quarters of an acre to maintain and grass that insists on growing at the most inconvenient times, you get creative. My solution? Goats.

Now, goats aren't just lawnmowers with legs, they've got personality. Among the handful we brought home was a little guy the kids named Spade. Spade was super cute, young, energetic, and friendly. The kids loved him.

But Spade had one quirk that set him apart: a serious identity crisis. He didn't think he was a goat at all. He was convinced he was *one of the dogs.* He followed them everywhere, napped beside them, and even learned to butt his head just enough to join in their games of tag. And when we discovered he was supplementing his diet with dog food while the dogs were happily munching on his grain. I figured that was about as "equal opportunity" as farm life gets.

But there was one thing Spade wanted more than anything: to go inside the house. The dogs could come and go as they pleased, and he wanted in on that club in the worst way. If he'd had opposable thumbs, he would've built himself a key.

Our days were busy. With three young kids running around, me working on converting the old horse stable into a woodworking shop, and everyone popping in and out all day long, it wasn't exactly Fort Knox around here. Spade watched, he plotted, and he waited. And eventually, his moment came.

I don't remember which one of us slipped up, but one afternoon, the door was left open just long enough. Next thing I knew, Spade was in the house, hooves clattering on the tile like a parade gone wrong.

Once that goat got inside, he was *untouchable.* He was faster than the kids, smarter than the dogs, and way too amused with himself to be caught. Spade pranced. Spade danced. Spade bounded. He knocked over chairs, shoved a side table into the wall, and scattered throw pillows like confetti. Attempting to herd him back out the door was like wrestling with a greased-up toddler on roller skates.

The only trick that worked, and I use "worked" loosely, was the mirror. See, Spade had one weakness. If he spotted a mirror, he'd freeze mid-chaos, his whole body going still as he locked eyes with his "new friend." That reflection was his long-lost twin, his partner in crime, his soulmate.

So, we'd herd him, one shuffle, sidestep, and dart at a time, toward the hallway mirror. The second he saw it, he'd stop cold, lean forward, and start his little goat conversation... soft bleats, nose nudges, the works. While he was distracted saying hello to his "buddy," we'd swoop in for the catch. By the time I wrestled him out the door, it looked like a tornado had passed through.

You'd think after a few of these rodeos, he'd stop sneaking in. Not Spade. He treated it like was his calling. Every open door was an opportunity.

And honestly, I couldn't blame him. He didn't see himself as a goat at all. He was just one of us, equal parts mischief and charm, determined to live the good life with his four-legged friends. Every now and then, I still think about that darn stubborn goat and all the joyful chaos he brought to our doorstep. Life was loud, unpredictable, and completely wonderful. I wouldn't trade a single hoofprint of it.

"Mirror, mirror in the hall... who's the friendliest goat of all?"

FOWL PLAY AT SUNRISE

It was the crack of dawn, that golden hour when the world whispers and stretches its sleepy arms. Except that morning, it wasn't whispers that woke me, it was honking. Loud, relentless honking!

Was I dreaming? Nope. I shuffled to the window, rubbing my eyes, and there it was: the neighbor's field, absolutely packed with Canadian Geese. Dozens? Hundreds? I couldn't count; it was a sea of black and white bodies with necks held high like tiny aristocrats.

Now, let me set the stage. This wasn't just any field. We'd recently weathered a once-in-a-century flood that turned the area into a marshy wasteland. Crops? Gone. Livelihoods? Wiped out. But Mother Nature, ever the opportunist, had transformed the soggy aftermath into a bird's buffet. The field had become an accidental sanctuary, hosting all sorts of feathered freeloaders.

But Canadian Geese? I'd never seen one in my life. And here they were, in the field next door! This was a moment meant for the ages. I leapt out of bed, grabbed my camera and shoes, and headed for the field faster than you can say "golden goose."

When I got close, I crouched low, crawling on hands and knees, one eye on the geese and the other on my camera, praying I wouldn't scare them off. Finding the perfect spot, I settled in, raised my camera, and clicked away.

Click. Click. Click. Oh, I was nailing it. These photos? Pulitzer-worthy. National Geographic was practically begging for them already. I paused to review my handiwork. That's when I saw it.

No. SIM. Card. The words stared back at me like a cruel joke. My jaw hit the mud. I'd just shot the best photos of my life, and my camera was about as useful as a rock.

Determined not to let this flock, or fate, get the better of me, I crawled back to the house, grabbed the SIM card, and hightailed it back to the field. To my relief, the geese were still there. Round two commenced.

This time, I got my pictures. Beautiful shots of their wings stretched wide, their glossy feathers catching the early light, and even a few squabbles over who had dibs on the prime patch of grass. It wasn't until later, when I Googled "Canadian Geese," that I discovered they can be aggressive little honkers. Apparently, getting too close can end in flapping, hissing, and outright attacks.

Good grief. I'd been sitting among them, obliviously, grinning like a fool. Either I had found the friendliest flock in existence, or Lady Luck had decided to keep me in one piece that day.

As it turned out, the geese weren't in any rush. They feasted on that field for a whole week. At first, their very early sunrise honking was charming, a natural alarm clock that made me feel like I lived in a Disney movie. By day seven? Not so much. Let's just say the charm wore off fast.

When they finally flew off, the quiet felt deafening. But every time I see one of those photos, I'm reminded of that wild week when the geese came to town and I learned two things:

Always check for a SIM card, and never underestimate a goose.

"Always check your camera before crawling into a goose convention."

WHERE TROUBLE GETS CAUGHT

I never planned to turn my garage into an art gallery. Honestly, it just sort of happened. When we moved to St. George, Utah, I needed a space to keep busy without quite so much risk to my fingers. Back in Waco, my workshop had been called *Trouble's Woodshop*—because, well, that's what it was. All sawdust, a table saw and other amazing tools, the kind of place that smells like cedar and determination.

But by the time we unpacked in Utah, I was 78 and not quite as interested in losing any fingers to "creative inspiration." I still loved making things, though, and I wanted a space where I could try some gentler projects. So the garage became the place for a few new hobbies: growing microgreens, dehydrating fruit and meat (because doing that inside the house made it smell too good and kept us up at 2 a.m.), and generally puttering with whatever struck my fancy.

We needed a new name for the space, something broader than "woodshop." When I posed the question to my son, he didn't even hesitate. "Trouble's Trap," he said.

We all laughed, and that was that. The name stuck. After all, it's the one place I can wander in, get lost for hours, and not feel the least bit guilty about it.

Before long, I found myself spending more time in the garage than anywhere else, tinkering, painting, rearranging, and working on little projects I swore would make life easier (or at least prettier).

One day I looked around and realized: that my life had spilled out into stacks of photos, old prints, little art projects, family snapshots, and more beagle pictures than any one person should have. And instead of hiding them away, I thought, why not hang them up where I can enjoy them.

And so, my garage doors became a memory wall filled with sixty years of life's adventures.

Each panel holds its own little corner of my history:

• **"Wild & Whimsical":** animals from farms, county fairs, horse motels, and wild parks — a proud parade of horses, donkeys, goats, elephants, and zebras, all captured mid-mischief.

• **"Family Ties":** snapshots of kids, grandkids, and family meals: the laughter, the awkward poses, the love, all frozen in time.

• **"Wanderlust & Wonder":** photographs from Japan, mountain valleys, bridges, rivers, and quiet moments that remind me how big and small the world can feel all at once.

• **"Beagle Chronicles":** Wilbee and Izzie, the ever-loyal comic relief — napping on pillows, stealing the spotlight, and teaching me that joy often comes with floppy ears.

• **"A Brush with Me":** my own paintings and sketches — landscapes, still lifes, and a few experiments that didn't go as planned but still make me smile.

Now, every time I step into *Trouble's Trap*, it feels like being greeted by my own personal museum. There's no admission charge, no velvet ropes—just the faint scent of wood and oil paint, sunlight sneaking through the window, and a chorus of memories waiting to say hello. Just a lifetime of moments staring back, saying, "Remember when?" And the beauty of this project is that I can change the artwork with other memories whenever I want to.

Visitors don't always know what to make of it. Some stand quietly, smiling at a photo or pointing to a familiar face; others just shake their heads and call it "so you."

But for me, it's the perfect reminder that a life well-lived is a little messy, a lot colorful, and always worth framing.

I've been lucky enough to live a life full of stories—and this is where a lot of them hang out.

THE FAMILY

Japanese Daily Life
In 1970
日常生活

Low Bar, Cleared with Style

I'm not supposed to say this, but buying a house can be a real crapshoot. Let's face it: Natalie and I bought and sold a few properties over the years, which means we'd seen our fair share of houses and neighbors.

When Natalie got a job in Baltimore, we started out as renters. Rent was pricey, though, and places hard to find, and Maryland's renter laws at the time weren't exactly friendly for the tenant. After just three months renting, we were ready to bolt. The landlady turned out to be our worst nightmare. The reasons don't matter now, but trust me, we were done.

So, we entertained the idea of buying a house. But after poking around Baltimore, it became painfully clear that anything we could afford would come with a side of leaky ceilings, broken windows, and missing walls, and questionable plumbing. Then we had a brilliant thought: in just an hour's drive, we'd be in Pennsylvania, where houses just over the border were much cheaper and livable. A realtor showed us a few properties, and soon enough, we were the proud owners of a house in Seven Valleys, Pennsylvania. That experience kicked off our new philosophy: if you're moving, buy, don't rent.

About two house purchases later, we landed our dream property in west Weber County, Utah, where we could finally build our little mini-farm. The location was great, the house had good bones (even if we had to fix it up), and we were thrilled.

Of course, every house comes with surprises, and ours showed up in the form of a pickup truck one sunny afternoon. I was in the front yard when the truck pulled up and out stepped a man who asked if I was the new owner. I told him I was. To my absolute shock, he said, "I love you."

Now, let me tell you, that's not the kind of thing you expect to hear from a stranger. My brain froze, and for some reason, the only thing I could think to say was, "What did these people do to you?"

Turns out, the previous lady of the house had been a bit on the crazy side. She had it out for this poor man, who regularly drove past the property. Whenever she saw his truck, she'd throw beer bottles into the road, so he'd have to drive over them. Who does that?

After this revelation, we started hearing more stories about the former owners. Let's just say their behavior hadn't exactly won them any popularity contests. Compared to them, we were practically saints. All we had to do to win over the neighbors was not sue them, not throw them in jail, and not call every authority under the sun with wild accusations. It was a low bar, but we cleared it with style.

When we eventually decided to sell the house and go on our RV walkabout, the neighbors begged us to sell to "nice people" like us. They even made half-joking threats about sabotaging any potential buyers they didn't approve of.

"If someone shady comes to look at the place, we'll make sure they see something they won't like," they said with a mischievous grin. I fired back, "If you keep doing that and someone still buys it, they're probably just like the last owners!"

There was even talk of putting our RV up on blocks so we couldn't leave. It's a special kind of heartwarming to know you're wanted, even if the "want" comes with a touch of mischief. Thankfully, the new owners turned out to be delightful, and the neighborhood remained its happy little self.

Here's the thing: buying a house is like rolling dice. You never really know what kind of neighborhood you're moving into. But in our experience, people are mostly pleasant. Sure, you'll occasionally stumble across someone who throws beer bottles in the road, but for the most part, neighbors just want to get along. And if you're lucky, they might even try to hold your RV hostage to keep you around a little longer.

SNOW JOB

When we lived in North Ogden, Utah, nestled up against the bench, winters weren't just winters, they were Winters with a capital W. Snow fell in such thick, fluffy blankets that it made you wonder if the clouds had just given up on the sky altogether and decided to live with us on the ground instead.

Now, at that time, we had built a custom sunroom with a flat roof that was attached to our house; just so we could enjoy our swim spa year-round. Oh, it was a fine setup, cozy and luxurious. But come winter, we discovered one critical flaw: flat roofs don't love snow. Twelve inches piling up might look charming and picturesque, but that kind of charm can also collapse a roof if you're not careful.

Lucky for us, we could access the roof through a second-floor bedroom window. One fine snowy day, with a good solid layer up there, we armed ourselves with shovels and climbed out onto the roof. Our mission: to clear the snow without taking an accidental dive off the edge. After much slipping, sliding, and shoving, we managed to scrape the roof clean. That's when we realized something.

We had dumped all that snow in one huge pile right along the building's walkway and door. Brilliant. So, after our first round of snow shoveling, we had to shovel again just to be able to exit the back of the house. Let me tell you, that kind of workout isn't for the faint of heart. By the time we finished, I felt like I'd just auditioned for the Olympic snow-shoveling team.

Naturally, we decided there had to be a better way. Enter the electric power snow shovel, a miraculous contraption that could shoot snow exactly where you wanted it to go. When the next big snowfall hit, we were ready. This time, with the power shovel in hand, we cleared the roof like pros and hurled the snow away from the building out toward the fence at the edge of our property. Problem solved, right?

Wrong. Later that day, we spotted one of our beagles tearing around the neighborhood like he'd just won the freedom lottery.

Now, our backyard was fenced, so this made no sense. Once we corralled the little escape artist, we followed him back into the yard to investigate. And that's when we saw it: our perfectly aimed pile of snow had formed a nice, sturdy ramp over the fence and straight into the neighbor's yard, which had no fence at all. The dog had taken one look at that icy highway to freedom and said, "Don't mind if I do!"

Of course, fixing that mess was easier said than done. The power snow shovel had compacted the pile-turned-ramp into a mini-iceberg. We had to chop, chip, and shovel until our backs were sore and our spirits were thoroughly humbled. Lesson learned: snow removal is an art, and mastering it comes with a few neck pains along the way.

By the time we'd cleared away that sneaky escape ramp and fine-tuned our snow-clearing strategy, we were ready to handle whatever Old Man Winter threw our way. And the rest of the season went off without a hitch—well, unless you count the time the blower decided to shoot snow straight at me instead of the fence. But that's another story.

"We mastered snow removal...right after the beagle mastered escape routes."

THE DAY WE GOOGLED 'SEX BOLT'

Back in the days when we ran our Construction Document Checking business, we came across a lot of industry-specific vocabulary. We worked on all kinds of commercial projects. What mattered was that everything matched up in the project documents. That's where the specifications, or "Specs", came in. They are the official instructions and ensure consistency, accuracy, and compliance with project requirements. Basically, the Specs tell you everything that the drawings can't—materials, dimensions, workmanship standards, you name it.

Since we handled a variety of projects, sometimes we'd see building types we hadn't run into before. But as long as everything aligned within the drawings and specs, we were good. Well… mostly good.

Now here comes the story.

One day, during a quiet work session, one of our reviewers suddenly shouted out a question:

"What is a sex bolt?"

The whole office froze. There were about four of us there that day, and every single one of us blinked like deer caught in awkward headlights. Surely, he was joking?

Someone piped up with "It must be a typo, hex bolt would be my guess." He wasn't sure and said he wanted to look it up. The internet wasn't exactly as good back then, and definitely not as safe for work. I hollered, "Hold on now! I don't want you to type that into a search bar on the business account! Lord knows what kind of ads or pictures we'll start getting after that!"

I won't lie. The images running through my head were not about door hardware.

Of course, our crew wasn't going to let this go. That night, one of our brave reviewers went home and did the research on his personal internet account. The next morning, he came in grinning like he'd cracked the Da Vinci Code.

A sex bolt, it turns out, is real hardware! It even has alternate names: Sex Bolt Mounting Screws, Mating Screws, Mating Fasteners… the list goes on.

They're used mainly to install things like kick-plates, panic bars, door closers, and hinges—especially in hollow doors. They add strength and security and make it easy to assemble from both sides. Just so you know what this type of bolt looks like, here is a picture.

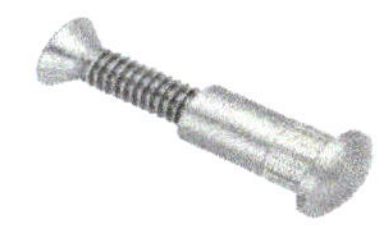

Honestly? I was impressed that our team cared enough to figure it out and share it. And yes, we had so much fun talking about it once we knew the truth. You can imagine.

Lesson learned: never underestimate what you'll learn in construction... or how red your face can get while doing it.

"Not every search term belongs on the company Wi-Fi."

CATCH THIS!

When people say, "College was the best time of my life," they usually mean keg stands and philosophy debates at 2 a.m. Me? I was 40-something and there I was in college. Yep. College. Me, a grown woman with three kids, a hefty rent bill, and a perfectly good library card, rooming with not one, but *two* of my children at the University of Utah.

Why? Because we were family. Because rent was cheaper when you share a bathroom. And because I'm not one to let my kids have all the fun, or all the ramen.

We had this lovely rhythm: Natalie, Kirk, and me, doing laundry, studying, making group dinners, and occasionally fighting over the last slice of garlic bread. Friends came by all the time, ours, theirs, mutuals—and the apartment was full of laughter, books, music, and the smell of microwave burritos.

One day, Kirk's buddy came by. Nice enough, fella. The kicker? He had a baby, six months old. Cute as a button. It smelled like talcum powder and warmed milk.

Now let me be honest. I've had babies. I've raised three. I love them deeply… but I am *not* what you'd call a "baby person." You know the type. They see a baby and turn into mashed potatoes. Me? I smile politely and make sure there's no spit-up coming my way.

Anyway, it was a beautiful day, and we were standing outside talking, like civilized folks. The baby was doing its little coo and smile routine, and we were just chatting. And then. Outta nowhere. No warning.

This boy, this father, takes his infant child, and with the confidence of a frat boy at a tailgate, launches that baby at Kirk.

LAUNCHED.

Not handed. Not nudged. Not "here, hold him for a sec." No, ma'am, this was a high pass. A full spiral. A tight throw. That baby left the father's hands like a Hail Mary on fourth and long.

Kirk, God love him, reacted like a pro. He caught that child midair, cradled it like a football that poops, and looked up at the baby's father with a face that said: *"Did you just THROW YOUR CHILD at me?!"*

Natalie and I stood there slack-jawed. I mean… what the hell just happened? Not a peep from the baby. Not a tear. Just big eyes like,

"Wheee!" Meanwhile Kirk is still trying to figure out if he just got punked or nearly became a character witness.

I snapped. Oh yes, I did. I said to that boy, loud and clear: "WHAT IF HE DIDN'T CATCH THE BABY?" And do you know what that fool said? *"Nobody's ever dropped him."*

Oh. Well. **EXCUSE ME.** So that's the parenting plan now? Infant trust-falls? Really?

Look, I understand parenting is hard. I understand dads do things differently. But tossing your baby like a beanbag at a barbecue? That's not edgy. That's idiotic. Being a parent is tough. But being that baby? That's the real challenge.

So next time you see a young parent trying something "new," maybe ask a few follow-up questions before you get drafted into the baby bowl. And for heaven's sake, if someone ever yells "Catch!" and it's followed by a *child*, react fast, stay calm, and pray your reflexes are better than your blood pressure.

"The baby's fine. My blood pressure? Absolutely not."

A Kiss for Christmas

Christmas is truly for the whole family, isn't it? Natalie and I were reminiscing the other day about one particularly memorable Christmas when we had a cute but very sneaky (and furry) member of the family.

We did our usual Christmas traditions: trimming the tree with hot chocolate in hand, and of course, a bone for the dog to keep him occupied while we hung ornaments. We sang "The Twelve Days of Christmas," badly, though I have to admit, our hound dog's contribution to the off-pitch harmony mostly involved tail thumping and a few off-tune howls. We counted him as part of the choir anyway.

The excitement built as Christmas Eve approached. The kids were bouncing with anticipation, sneaking peeks at the presents under the tree, trying to guess what each one might be. And back then, we made sure everyone had a gift under the tree, even the dog. He usually got his bone wrapped up in festive paper so he could join the unwrapping chaos.

At the last minute that year, I decided to add a little surprise: the kids' favorite treat, a giant chocolate Kiss, the kind you only see around Christmas, wrapped up shiny and bright. It went right under the tree with the rest of the gifts. Satisfied with my cleverness, I headed off to bed, knowing full well I'd be up early with kids hollering and bouncing on my bed before sunrise.

Christmas morning, the kids stormed into the living room ready to attack the presents. But before we even got started, I spotted something odd under the tree. All that remained of my clever surprise was a crumpled bit of foil, no chocolate Kiss in sight. Sitting nearby was one very guilty-looking dog, doing his best to look innocent while his tail wagged nervously.

The kids were not impressed.

While he still happily accepted his Christmas bone like nothing had happened, the look on his face told the real story. That dog knew exactly what he had done, and he wasn't even a little bit sorry. After all, I've yet to meet a dog that's ever truly felt guilty about anything. Thankfully, the chocolate didn't seem to bother him (we all kept a close eye on him for a while), but I learned my lesson: Never, and I do mean never, put food under the Christmas tree. Ever.

Looking back now, it still makes me laugh. It was one of those perfectly imperfect family moments that make holidays memorable. That Christmas might've cost me a giant chocolate Kiss, but it gave us a story we've told for years.

"Christmas morning: some assembly required, some chocolate missing."

MARINARA, MUSICALS, AND A MORMON

After Natalie and I moved back to Ogden, Utah, we started settling into our new community. We were living out in the Weber County farmland, surrounded by sweet people, quiet views, and cows that looked like they'd seen some things.

One evening, we attended a local caucus meeting. It was one of those civic events where you vote for your district delegates, but mostly it was a chance to meet the neighbors. After the meeting, we mingled, and I struck up a conversation with a man I'd never met before. Nice guy. Friendly. Chatty.

Then, out of the blue, he asked if we'd do him a favor. Now, when someone leads with that and you've only known him twelve minutes, you brace yourself.

He explained that in the local Mormon tradition, teenagers approaching missionary age are sometimes sent to families in the community for "cultural dinner nights." It's a way for them to practice encountering different customs, sort of like missionary dress rehearsals. You were to act like you were in another country and feed them accordingly.

He asked if we'd host a dinner for his daughter and her friend. He said we could pick the country.

I was stunned. He didn't know a thing about us! And here he was, handing over his precious daughter for an evening in a stranger's home to be shown "how other people live."

Well, how could I say no?

I asked, "Would you like Italy or Japan?" I'd lived in both, but figured Italy was the safer bet. Japanese cuisine might've been a bit too adventurous, and I didn't want to serve sushi while kneeling on the floor like a rogue yoga instructor.

So: Italy. The menu? A modest little 30-course extravaganza.

When the girls arrived, their father dropped them off like they were attending prom, with scriptures. They were dressed up, holding their Books of Mormon like shields, and looked unsure about the evening ahead.

I smiled sweetly and said, "Welcome to Italy! May I offer you a glass of wine?"

The look on their faces! Absolute horror. One of them gasped and blurted out before thinking, "We don't drink alcohol." Missionary reflexes in action.

"Oh, I know," I said, still smiling. "But you're in *Italy*. Here, almost every family makes their own wine, by hand, with pride. To refuse it outright can really offend your host."

You could see them freeze like deer in the spotlight. I added gently, "Now, I absolutely respect your religious beliefs. I really do. But this is one of those moments missionaries face all over the world—how do you say, 'no thank you' in a way that honors *your* values *and* the local culture?"

That, right there, is the missionary starter pack: cultural respect with personal integrity. If you can navigate that without offending your host or compromising your faith, you're on your way.

One of the girls took a breath and said, "It smells lovely… but no thank you. It's against our religion, but we're grateful to be here."

I nodded like a proud auntie. "Very good. And now, on to the spaghetti!" Once we got past that moment, everything softened. They relaxed. Within fifteen minutes, they were laughing, twirling pasta, and happily chatting about the high school musicals they were starring in.

Somewhere between the meatballs and the tiramisu, Natalie asked how school was going. That cracked the lid on something deeper.

They were frustrated. "It's just so hard for us to get good grades," one of them said. "It's not fair, it's like the smart kids don't even have to try."

Oh, honey. That hit a familiar nerve. So, we set down our forks and had a full-on kitchen table heart-to-heart.

We asked, "Should rewards be based on effort or results?"

"When you go to a doctor, or hop on a plane, do you care how hard the person *tried*, or how well they actually did?"

They paused. That one landed.

But then we flipped the script: "What if those straight-A kids were asked to get on a stage, sing in front of a crowd, or lead a group emotionally through something hard? Could they do that?"

They thought about it.

We said, "Your gifts may not show up on a test, but they matter just as much." Then we asked the big one: "Would you trade your strengths to have someone else's?" They both shook their heads.

"No. I like who I am," one of them said. And that was it. Their whole posture changed. You could see how the pressure lifted off their shoulders.

Not long after, whether it was the pasta, the pep talk, or just the energy in the room, they stood up and announced they would like to do a performance for us. Natalie and I looked at each other and grinned. "Of course you do," I said.

They dove in like seasoned Broadway veterans, singing, dancing, and even doing a bit of improv theater. They made up their own little musical on the spot. Half *Joseph and the Amazing Technicolor Dreamcoat*, half *Sound of Music*, with a dash of jazz hands and zero hesitation.

We gave them a standing ovation and hollered for an encore. They were more than happy to oblige, launching into a duet that gave me chills and made Natalie tear up. Who knew a couple of modest Mormon girls could bring the house down like that?

Then the doorbell rang. Dad had arrived. They looked like they'd been caught sneaking out the back door of a speakeasy.

And let me tell you, we got the fastest spiritual lesson in the history of the church. It was like a TED Talk on 2x speed: testimony, scriptures, a brief parable, and a thank-you all in under three minutes.

Before he left, I handed him a neatly packed doggy bag of Italian leftovers. "Just so the rest of the family can try the meal," I said. "Figured you'd want to know what we fed these young ladies."

I guess we did okay. Because the next year, we were asked to host the girl's twin brother. He went home raving. Said it was the best night he'd ever had. The year after that, their third kid arrived—and told us *she'd* been waiting for *her* turn. By then, this "cultural dinner" was turning into an annual tradition.

And then came the fourth and youngest. Poor girl. Just when her year came around, we were packing up to move. We were moving into an RV, full time, to travel the country.

When the family heard that, they practically begged us to stay just *one more month* so their daughter could have her Italian night. They even offered to let us park the RV on their property until she got her turn.

Now that's what I call emotional blackmail — served with a breadstick. And honestly, I was touched. We were just doing what anyone would do: opening the door, making a plate of food, and letting kids stretch into something bigger than their comfort zone.

Besides, my youngest had converted and gone on a mission himself. So, I knew firsthand just how important it was to show a little kindness, a little culture, and a lot of carbs.

"One glass of wine, two missionaries, and a lesson in culture."

Do You Do Everything Your Mother Taught You?

Back in Miami, when I was in junior high, schools were packed tighter than a church potluck. We had six classes a day, barely enough desks, and nowhere near enough textbooks.

My math class in particular was a circus. The teacher was a man I will generously call "Mr. Pembroke S. Stiffman," because, if ever a man looked like he starched his soul every morning, it was him. He typically sat on a tall barstool at the front of the room and lectured at us like we were all magically absorbing his words through osmosis.

Spoiler: we weren't.

Without books or anything to follow along with, it was like listening to a radio with no knob, just one long unchanging buzz of misery. I got bored. I mean drooling-on-the-desk, counting-the-ceiling-tiles, trying-to-keep-my-eyes-open bored.

To stay awake, I did what any reasonable Trouble-in-Training would do. I whispered with the other kids. Not full-blown gossip, just enough chatter to keep my brain from going completely numb.

Well, Mr. Stiffman didn't like that. Not one bit.

One day, mid-mumble, he stopped his lecture cold. Dead silent. The room froze.

Then, in his best dramatic voice, he said to me: "Is that what your mother taught you to do? Talk while your teacher is teaching?"

Without thinking, I shot back: "No sir! Do you do everything your mother taught you to do?"

Dead. Silence.

You could feel the whole room tighten, waiting to see if I'd survive the next 30 seconds. A few desks creaked. Someone behind me let out a gasp.

Now, in our school, everybody knew Mr. Stiffman didn't raise his voice. He didn't have to. One hard stare from him could make a cockroach rethink its life choices. So, when I said those words, the whole class reacted like I'd just poked a sleeping alligator.

The boy next to me scooted his chair two full inches away, like sarcasm was contagious. The girl in front reached over and squeezed my hand in a quiet little "good luck, soldier." Even the class lizard who wasn't an official class pet, just something that lived behind the chalkboard, stuck his head out like he wanted to witness the carnage.

Then, boom! The room exploded. Not literally, but with noise. Laughter, whispers, a mix of admiration and panic. Mr. Stiffman turned redder than cafeteria spaghetti sauce.

And guess what? That class was right before lunch.

Guess who didn't get lunch that day?

The whole class.

He kept us in the room, standing in silent punishment like we were in a courtroom. I'm not proud that everyone went hungry... but I'm also not that sorry.

Lesson of the day? If you're going to talk back, be prepared to sacrifice your pizza square.

Was it worth it? Yeah. It kinda was.

"Respect your elders… unless they're boring and sitting on a barstool."

MINOR INCIDENT INVOLVING PANIC

Every place has its claim to fame. South Dakota has Mount Rushmore. Rome has the Colosseum. Utah has the Great Salt Lake. When I lived in Japan, our little town of Hayama had something too. It wasn't a landmark, though it definitely left an impression. It had legs. Lots of 'em. And it wasn't particularly polite.

Our little neighborhood was known for one thing: the Ashidakagumo, Japan's largest species of wandering spider. We just called them *Hayama Spiders.* Imagine something the size of your palm… or worse, your face. And they move supper fast. Olympic fast. Ninja fast.

One quiet afternoon, I was reading on the couch, completely relaxed, when I heard a strange ticking noise. It got louder, like something skittering. I looked up, and there it was. The largest, ugliest spider I'd ever seen. Just right there beside my head on the wall, like it paid rent.

I panicked. Rolled right off the couch and stared at the beast, eyes wide, heart hammering, dignity gone. My husband? At work. Natalie? Safe in bed for her nap. Me? Clearly on my own in this horror film.

I did what any reasonable woman would do. I ran next door to get my landlady. She was kind and curious and extremely Japanese. I mimed the situation with dramatic hand motions. Crawling spider. My house. Big panic.

She gasped, sucked air through her teeth in horror, then disappeared into her house. I thought, oh good, she's going to return with backup. No such luck. She came back with a tiny spray can and something that looked like a toy fly swatter. She pantomimed: spray, smack, done. I stood there thinking, this isn't a fruit fly. This is a demon with legs. Still, I thanked her (politely, of course) and returned home to kill the beast myself.

Except it was gone. That psychic spider *knew* I was coming back armed. It had vanished into some crevice in the universe, leaving me with nothing but the creeping certainty that it was *still in the house.* Watching. Waiting.

Days passed. Then weeks. I almost convinced myself it was a fever dream. Until one night… in our tatami room, I spotted it again.

There on the wall. That same palm-sized monster, watching me like it had unfinished business.

My husband was *again* at work (convenient), but I had my tools. I sprayed the hell out of it. Just coated that sucker until it looked like a frosted mini-wheat. Then I raised the fly swatter… but I just couldn't do it. I couldn't splatter it across a wall I couldn't properly clean. That had permanent nightmare written all over it.

But the spider wasn't done. It shook like the devil had sneezed on it. The frost flew off. It bolted across the wall and disappeared behind the silk screen, the exact silk screen that hung right over our heads when we laid our futons down at night.

Absolutely not. I worked up the courage to lift the screen. Behind it, I saw the spider, crumpled, one leg stuck to the screen. It looked dead. But just as I moved to clean it up, it dropped to the floor—alive—and stopped cold in the middle of the room.

It just sat there. Not dead. Not moving. Mocking me.

I wasn't about to squish that thing on tatami matting. That floor is sacred and impossible to clean. So, I did what any practical, half-terrified, slightly unhinged woman would do. I grabbed my 3-wood golf club, opened the sliding doors to the great outdoors, walked up to that spider, smiled and took a full swing.

Fore! Problem solved.

"My landlady gave me a toy and a prayer. I brought the 3-wood."

DAD IN THE SPEAKER

When my husband deployed to Vietnam for a year, I became the whole home team: referee, coach, cheerleader, and cleanup crew. Our son was 15 months old, our daughter 28 months, and baby number three was just three months on the way. We were a tiny circus, and I was the ringmaster whether I felt ready or not.

Now, I've always believed kids need their father, and fathers need to see their kids, especially at those magic ages where they seem to grow into completely different people every other week. So I photographed everything: playground sand fights, beach days, toddler tantrums, first haircuts, scraped knees, birthday cupcakes, you name it. I stuffed pictures into letters until the envelopes bulged. But as far as the kids were concerned, Daddy was… theoretical. A name, a concept, a rumor.

Then we found our secret weapon: the stereo system. A glorious piece of equipment back then: record player, reel-to-reel, and cassette deck. Their father started sending voice recordings home, and everything changed.

Whenever a new tape arrived, the kids stretched out on the carpet, pressed their little hands against the speakers, and listened like tiny disciples receiving scripture. That faraway voice became a presence. They called the speaker "Daddy." If the machine warmed up, they'd pat it, whisper to it, or toddle over and give it updates on their day. As far as they knew, Daddy lived inside the box.

Six months later, baby number three arrived. Not long after, the Navy granted Hubby a one-week leave. He walked through that front door bone-tired but glowing.

The kids froze.

They stared. Blinked. Tilted their heads in unison like confused puppies. Who was this man? Why was he in our living room?

And, most suspicious of all, why did he sound exactly like Speaker Daddy?

We told them this was Daddy, the same one who talked from the box. They listened, but their squinty little expressions said, *"But… why isn't he in the speaker where he belongs?"*

And let me tell you, having him home that week was not the Hallmark moment people imagine. Our little household had a routine. A rhythm. A way of functioning without Daddy. And here comes this tall stranger trying to make rules, give orders, and perform what he called "discipline," which was a foreign concept to two toddlers who'd been in charge for months.

Todd, all 15 months of stubborn independence, took one look at this new guy telling him what to do and walked right up and kicked him hard in the shins. No hesitation. No fear. Just: *Don't interrupt my life, sir.*

Hubby went back to Vietnam with a bruise and a much clearer understanding of his place in the toddler hierarchy.

Six more months of Speaker Daddy followed before he finally returned home for good, duffel bag on his shoulder and hope in his eyes. And yes, it took time—real time—for three little people to accept Daddy in the flesh rather than Daddy in the furniture.

But slowly, the voice in the box became the man at the dinner table. The stranger became familiar. The shins stopped getting kicked. And bedtime stories, hugs, and tickle fights did the kind of bonding that no letter or tape could ever match.

That's how it goes, in the real world. Families don't snap together like puzzle pieces. Sometimes you have to teach the toddlers that Daddy is not, in fact, a household appliance.

But we got there.

And eventually, our family was whole again, shin bruises healed, speakers quiet, and Daddy exactly where he belonged.

They didn't know where Daddy was exactly.
They just knew his voice lived in the box.

Earthquake at the Worst Time

There are some moments in life that test your poise, your timing, and your paper walls. Living in Japan in the 1970s came with its share of surprises: surprise dinner guests, surprise weekends away, and in my case… surprise tectonic activity. Now, I've hosted my fair share of impromptu gatherings and navigated plenty of tricky situations, but nothing prepares a woman for an earthquake at the wrong time.

Back then, as a Navy officer's wife, life was... different. No one had telephones. They were too expensive and getting one could take a year or more.

That meant when the men decided at work, "Let's get together for dinner tonight," we wives wouldn't know until they showed up home with another couple in tow. And suddenly it was, "Surprise! Company's here. Time to kick your kitchen magic into high gear and whip up something impressive."

Fortunately, I had learned to batch-cook elegant homemade "TV dinners" and keep them frozen, ready for a moment just like this. If it looked like more than eight people were about to cram into my home, the standing rule was simple: bring your own food and booze, because I wasn't running a pop-up diner for the whole Navy.

We even had a system for spontaneous weekends. The couples with kids got their mama-sans to babysit, then we started making rounds. One friend's house, then another—hoping someone was home. If not, we'd catch them at the next house. And when enough of us gathered? The party would bloom.

Food came out, bottles opened, someone pulled out a guitar. We'd sit around the low table on the tatami mats, eating, drinking, laughing, and occasionally solving world problems between bites.

One particular night, we were deep into the merriment when I slipped away to use the restroom. Now, "restroom" is a generous term. In this house, the toilet was in a cubicle. A little wooden box along the hallway with a sliding paper door and just enough room to turn around if you weren't wearing a coat.

I shut the door behind me and just as I sat down—the whole world started shaking. Not metaphorically. Literally. The walls trembled. The floor buzzed. The entire tiny box shook like a tin can in a tumbling dryer. And there I was, pants down, bracing myself against the walls, praying they wouldn't collapse under my elbows. Then, just as suddenly, it stopped. Earthquake. Not a huge one, but enough to knock your balance and your pride sideways.

I made my way back to the party, acting as casual as a woman who just survived seismic movement on a toilet can act. That's when the comments started.

Laughingly someone asked, "What the heck were you *doing* in there?" Did you cause the earthquake?! Don't ever eat that much again, we can't handle the fallout!"

Now, I don't get embarrassed easily. But I have to say—if I can move the earth by taking a bathroom break, then I think I deserve a little teasing and a round of applause.

There's a certain kind of grace required to rejoin a party like nothing happened after riding out an earthquake in a glorified wooden closet. And if grace isn't available, then humor will do just fine. Life doesn't always give you warnings — it gives you stories, sometimes shaking and all. And if those stories happen to begin with a tremor and end with laughter, well… that's just the Trouble way.

"Turns out, I can bring down the house. Just not on purpose."

Floods, Sandbags & Helicopters

You ever have one of those days where it sounds like a NASCAR rally outside, but it turns out it's just the neighbors prepping for the end of the world? Yeah. That was us.

We lived on this little one-road neck of the woods where excitement usually means a raccoon trying to steal your lunch. So, when I saw a small army of three- and four-wheelers buzzing like caffeinated wasps down the neighbor's long dirt road, I did what any self-respecting woman with her own three-wheeler would do: I grabbed my keys and followed the chaos.

At the end of the road, ten men were digging like their lives depended on it. Shovels, sandbags, water everywhere. "The river's flooding," one said. I blinked. "What river?"

Turns out, we lived just a field or so away from a river that was feeling particularly emotional that week. It was spring, or close enough to it, and the mountains had gone from snowy postcard to overflowing bathtub. Our irrigation system wasn't ready, the fields weren't ready, and sure as hell, *we* weren't ready.

By the afternoon, our quiet view had turned into something that looked like a scene from *Waterworld*. That peaceful farmland turned into a lake. That road I drove my three-wheeler down? Turned itself into a river. My neighbor's tractor was now an aquatic exhibit.

But we adapted. Well… sort of. Let's call it "organized panic." Out came the backhoe—our new favorite toy. My daughter-in-law, fresh from flood-prone Winnipeg, brought wisdom from the north: proper sandbagging, ditch-digging, berm-building, and what I now call *Canadian Flood Engineering*. We had pipes to relieve pressure from the dirt walls, pumps to cycle water like a nervous casino fountain, and plastic tarps thicker than the plot of a telenovela.

FEMA arrived. News crews swarmed. A helicopter with a sandbag the size of a compact car flew *directly* over our roof, and then returned "empty handed" to do it again and again. And when the military rolled into the graveyard the next property over like a very somber action movie, well, I just poured myself a glass of wine and accepted that the apocalypse had found us.

The real kicker? It happened again. A second "hundred-year flood" in *six weeks*. At that point, I started checking the clouds for biblical horsemen.

Eventually, the water receded, leaving behind a community that had bonded over trench warfare, canoe accidents, and watching massive backhoes pull actual *trucks* out of the river. Tourists came to canoe in the temporary lake. The geese moved in and made it a resort. The farmers, bless 'em, probably cried into their crop-insurance paperwork.

And us? We sat at the edge of the flood zone—high and dry, thanks to our very lucky elevation, our hasty backhoe trench, and the graveyard acting like a divine sponge.

If FEMA shows up twice in one year, you're not doing something right, you're living next to a river with a grudge.

"Most folks dream of lakefront property, mine unexpectedly appeared."

A Roadside Dip to Remember

Some days, motherhood is about discipline, structure, and keeping everything neat and proper. Other days, it's about flinging the rulebook out the window.

It was one of those Beaufort, South Carolina days when the air sits heavy on your skin and your clothes feel like they've been glued in place. My girlfriend and I had decided to take the kids sightseeing. We headed to Savannah—because truth be told, Beaufort's tourist spots aren't exactly overflowing unless you happen to be into swamps, marshes, and a whole lot of "don't ask what's making that sound."

We'd just wrapped up the day and were headed back, forty minutes in my old faithful 1963 VW Bussie. She had a lot of charm and exactly zero air conditioning. At best, you got a warm breeze that felt like someone breathing on you after jogging uphill.

The kids were in full meltdown mode; sweaty, cranky, and radiating the kind of misery that could boil over into sibling warfare at any second. Then, my girlfriend spotted a skinny state road bridge and the dirt track leading down to the water.

She looked at me and half-joked, "We could just go jump in the river to cool off."

Half-joke was all I needed. I veered off like I'd been waiting for this all day. We rattled down the dirt road, found a shady spot under the bridge, and there it was: the river, looking like salvation.

Swimsuits? Not a chance. This was strictly sightseeing attire. But we weren't about to roast for another twenty something miles. So, without ceremony, I told the kids to strip to their underwear and get in. And in we went.

My girlfriend, who was always the "responsible" one, decided she'd "stand guard" to make sure no one came down the road. I'm fairly sure the real reason was she didn't want to be caught in her slip in broad daylight.

We splashed. We laughed. We forgot about the heat. The kids stopped fussing and started shrieking with joy instead. For those few minutes, we weren't just cooling off. We were living a little louder, a little freer.

The funniest part was how quickly the kids' attitudes changed. Ten minutes earlier, they'd been acting like we were dragging them through the seventh circle of sightseeing hell. But the moment their toes hit that cool water, suddenly they were wilderness explorers, river dolphins, and Olympic splash champions. Amazing what a little mud and freedom can do for children's souls.

Later that week, someone asked what we'd done for fun. I just smiled and said, "Oh, you know… took the kids sightseeing and accidentally baptized them in the river." Southern mothers nodded like that explained everything.

It wasn't in any parenting manual, and it sure wasn't in the day's itinerary. But those moments—the ridiculous, impulsive, barefoot ones—are the ones that stick. Years later, we still remember the day we pulled over, stripped down, and let a muddy river turn misery into magic. Sometimes, you just have to jump in.

"When the kids start steaming, toss 'em in the nearest river. Works every time."

WHAT'D YOU DO THAT FOR?

When I moved my little crew to Ogden, Utah, it was mostly for the fresh start and to be closer to my sister and her husband Jim, who just so happened to be an emergency room doctor.

Now, I don't want to say having a doctor in the family is the best thing ever… but it really is.

As it turned out, we were a pretty healthy bunch. We only needed Jim once for something ordinary, the time we all caught a stomach flu so vicious we were huddled around the one bathroom like campers sharing a single campfire in a blizzard. I called Jim and begged for help. He sent in a prescription that plugged us up like corks in wine bottles. Problem solved.

But most of the time, I didn't need Jim for illness. I needed him for the injuries I inflicted on myself.

Let me walk you through some of the highlights.

Powder Jacket

First, there was the powder jacket incident. You know the kind, it pulls over your head and zips up with a zipper the size of a garage door chain. I was in my usual rush, yanking the thing off over my head, when that big metal zipper pull rammed itself straight up my nose.

I swear, I thought I'd punctured my brain. Blood poured everywhere.

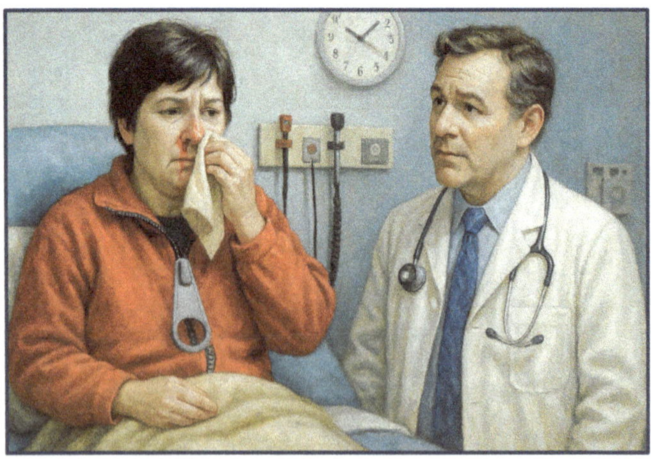

So, I marched into the emergency room holding a blood soaked towel to my face like a crime scene reenactment. When I told Jim what happened, he just looked at me and said, **"What'd you do that for?"**

I went home and considered burning the jacket, but I took it to a thrift store instead — with a note pinned to it that read, *"Warning: This jacket may be hazardous to your health."*

Woodshop

Next came the woodshop incident.

I was deep in a project when Natalie came in to ask a question. Now, you know me, I talk with my hands. I can't express myself with my arms hanging down like laundry. Unfortunately, one of those hands was holding a screwdriver. And during a particularly impassioned gesture, I stabbed myself right in the eye.

My eye turned bright red, like a police siren.

Back to the emergency room. The check-in nurse didn't even ask why I was there — apparently, my reputation had preceded me. When Jim saw me, he knew what happened before I said a word. Still, I felt compelled to explain. He sighed, shook his head, and said, **"What'd you do that for?"**

Golf

I could stop there. I should stop there. But let me give you just one more just for flavor.

I had married into a golfing family, complete with a father-in-law who was a teaching pro, and a husband who was a golf enthusiast. Naturally, learning to play became part of my life. I'd already taught my eldest son to play, and he was good, too good. If *he* had hit the ball that day, I probably wouldn't be here telling this story. This time, it was my younger son's turn to learn. He and a friend from junior high were eager, full of energy, and short on aim, so we spent plenty of afternoons at the little par-three course down the road.

One beautiful afternoon, they begged me to come along "just to coach and enjoy the sunshine." And of course, I said yes. The air smelled like cut grass and sunscreen, the boys were laughing and bragging, and I felt a little teacher's pride watching them improve.

Golf's supposed to be a game of patience and focus, but with two junior-high boys, it's mostly a game of noise management and luck. On one hole, I don't know what I was thinking. I wandered a bit ahead and crouched behind a tree, maybe forty-five degrees off the tee box.

My son hit a clean shot. Then his friend stepped up. He always took a few practice swings, and because I was watching, he took more than usual. Finally he settled, took a breath, and swung.

I peeked out from behind the tree to watch. After all, I was the teacher. Terrible idea.

He took a grand full swing and put his whole heart, soul, and maybe a little panic into it. BAM.

He shanked it directly into my Adam's apple. Knocked me flat. I thought I'd been hit by a rocket.

Not deadly, but it stung like the devil. The boys froze—two statues with golf clubs. Then they bolted toward me like they'd just seen a ghost. I tried to wave them off, but all that came out was a raspy "I'm fine!" which sounded more like a frog choking on a kazoo. Their eyes were huge; I think they thought they'd just committed manslaughter by Titleist. My throat started to swell, so I shuffled to the pro shop, one hand on my neck, the other clutching my pride. The man behind the counter took one look at me, winced, and said, "Bet you didn't see that shot coming." I couldn't even answer—too busy trying to breathe and glare at the same time. Then I drove home one-handed, one on the wheel, the other holding ice to my throat.

I called Jim and told him what happened. He sighed and said, **"What'd you do that for?"**

I could barely talk for two days, and the boys apologized for a week. But the next time we went golfing, they both aimed a little straighter—and I stayed way *behind* the tee box.

Now, I may be accident-prone. Sure, I might be a walking exhibit of *How Not to Do That*. But I've also had a life full of laughs, love, a doctor in the family, and a story for every scar.

And somehow, through it all, I've survived myself.

Cheeky Business in Italy

Let me start by saying this: Italians love babies and toddlers. They don't just smile at them. They don't just coo. They *attack.*

Not in a malicious way, mind you, this is an all-out affectionate ambush. A full-contact sport of cultural admiration.

Now picture me, a young American mom in the 1970s, still learning the rhythm of a new country, walking the cobblestone streets of a sun-soaked Italian town. Laundry flaps from balconies. The air smells like espresso and warm bread. I've got a baby strapped to my chest like a papoose, a toddler clinging to my hand, and one more hovering close enough to be in striking distance, when, right on cue, they descend.

"Che bella bambina!" they cry, hands already reaching.

And then, pinch.

Not a gentle tap, either. No, this was full commitment. They'd grab both cheeks and twist like they were testing the ripeness of a peach. Sometimes one woman, sometimes a whole pack of them, all laughing, cooing, and calling out blessings to my "beautiful children."

My poor kids never stood a chance. Natalie would duck behind my leg. Todd would scowl. And little Kirk, bless him, just froze like a deer in the headlights. One day, before the woman even touched her, Natalie screamed. I mean, a *preemptive scream.* Like a baby war veteran.

The Nonna just laughed, waving a hand. "È amore!" she said. It's love. Love? Ma'am, that's not love, that's a *cheek assault.*

I tried to be culturally sensitive. I really did. I read guidebooks. I practiced my polite Italian phrases. I wanted to fit in! But there's no chapter on "How to Remove *a* grandmother from Your Toddler's Face."

Once, I had to physically pry a woman's hands off Natalie's cheeks. She looked offended, like I'd interrupted a sacred ritual.

And if you thought you could hide in a café? Forget it. The owner's cousin's aunt would come out from the kitchen, wiping her hands on her apron, ready to pinch and bless and squeeze.

Eventually, I gave up trying to stop it. I started treating cheek-pinching like hail in spring, unpleasant, unpredictable, and best endured with a smile and the understanding that resistance only encouraged them.

Every once in a while, a Nonna would get particularly enthusiastic and go in for a full ninety-degree twist. The kids would come away dazed, cheeks blazing like stoplights, and I swear you could see the imprint of her fingers for an hour. I started carrying a little tin of cold cream in my purse. Not for me. For the children. For cheek triage.

The kids survived. Their cheeks bounced back.

But to this day, if you say "Nonna" near Natalie, she instinctively covers her face.

Some things leave a mark, emotionally and epidermally.

"They called it affection. My kids called it trauma."

ANGELS AMONG US

January 20, is a date that will always be remembered in our family. It's when we lost Ellie, my precious granddaughter. Life has carried on, as life tends to do, but the lessons Ellie taught us continue to endure, lessons of love, kindness, and joy, and will stay with us until the day we join her again.

At the time of her passing, one of Ellie's dear friends, a grown-up who had been deeply touched by her sweet spirit, asked me to write a tribute to honor Ellie's life and the light she brought into this world.

What poured out of me that day was both heartbreak and faith, wrapped together in the only way my heart knew how to speak. This is that piece, written for her then, and held close by us ever since.

I Believe

"When a child of almost seven years dies, we ask why? Behind every tear, bouquet of flowers, and condolence card is that haunting question WHY!

Not only was Ellie a beautiful, intelligent, and self-confident little girl. She was also filled with the ability to love beyond all measure. In these hard times since her death, we've discovered, again and again, just how many lives she touched with her pure and open heart.

So, I ask myself the hard question: Why did my grand-daughter Ellie die?

I believe God loves his children on the Earth and sometimes, He sends angels to live among us to teach us how to love one another.

I believe Ellie to be one of those very special angels. Her purpose was to show everyone that she met the purity, joy, comfort, and closeness of loving relationships. It was as natural as breathing to her.

But perhaps, to truly recognize Ellie's extraordinary gift, we had to be shaken awake. The unthinkable had to happen for us to stop taking her presence—and her lessons—for granted.

Through Ellie's friendship and love, we can learn many lessons:

To look upon others as friends and not strangers.

To accept others for who they are.

To leave notes of endearment, encouragement and love.

Be interested in what others are doing but also cherish simply having them near.

To treat each moment, with someone as if they're the "best"; the best friend, the best uncle, the best aunt, the best dad, the best mom, the best coach, you get the idea.

To share hearty belly laughs.

To give hugs freely and frequently.

To give 100% percent when doing anything, whether it's soccer, swimming, neighborhood concerts, video production, performing in gymnastics, or simply loving someone.

These are just a few of the lessons that come to mind. I'm sure that there will be many more as time goes by. All these acts of kindness and love from Ellie are now priceless gifts that we will treasure.

In a short lifetime, Ellie had completed her task. It was time this angel to return to the heaven, to be ready for the next assignment that God has for her to bless others with her divine gift.

However, her work isn't finished with us. Let us learn and live these lessons she taught us every day for the rest of our lives. We thank the Lord for sending us Ellie."

Even today, Ellie's messages live on. My son, inspired by her legacy, created a non-profit organization called "Ellie's Way." Its mission is to provide comfort, encouragement, and hope to those who are grieving. Ellie's light continues to shine, helping others heal. I see Ellie's message growing stronger in our hearts.

We can love one another.

GINGER ALE GEYSER GAMES

Before the divorce, our little family had spent several years living overseas while my husband served in the Navy. Japan, then Italy: both wonderful, both full of memories, and both full of *really good* beer. So when life brought the kids and me back to the States afterward, I quickly learned that American beer tasted like fizzy disappointment. I wanted something hearty, flavorful, something worth the bubbles. So, I did what any determined, slightly stubborn woman would do: I learned to brew my own.

It started with beer, of course. Natalie and I became a two-woman brewery. The boys weren't interested, which suited me fine. Fewer hands in the hops meant fewer mouths on the bottles.

We studied sugar levels, yeast behavior, temperatures, and timing. We bought proper bottles, none of those flimsy, explode-in-your-closet nonsense. Our beer room stayed cool and calm, much like us on bottling day, and after a few months, we had brews that could put some microbreweries to shame.

Then came the soda phase.

I figured if we could make beer, surely, we could whip up a batch of ginger ale. Something for the boys: sweet, bubbly, and harmless. So, I gathered the ingredients, cooked the syrup, washed and filled the bottles.

But the beer had already claimed our precious cool room. So, the ginger ale found a new home, in the basement, tucked next to the old octopus-style heating system.

A decision that may not have been the wisest. Foreshadowing? Absolutely.

Three months later, it was time for the grand opening. Natalie grabbed a bottle, popped the cap with flair, and *Old Faithful erupted.*

A perfect, powerful geyser of ginger ale shot to the kitchen ceiling and rained sticky droplets across every surface we owned.

We stared in shock. Then we howled with laughter.

"Try another one!" I said. But not inside — once was enough.

So we headed outside to keep the mess where nature could deal with it. The next bottle blew just as spectacularly. Then another. And another. The kids took turns opening them, one at a time. But the real fun started once we discovered a fascinating bit of backyard physics:

If you covered the opening with your thumb and shook the bottle hard, you could *aim* the resulting enhanced spray. It was a sticky, sweet, ginger-scented water cannon. Well, that changed everything.

The yard turned into a soda battlefield. The kids ran across the grass with bottles fizzing in their hands, spraying each other from behind trees like carbonated snipers. Someone shrieked. Someone slipped. Someone else declared himself King of Ginger Ale Mountain. By the end, all three children were soaked, giggling, and thoroughly glazed in sugar.

The ginger ale was a total failure. But the afternoon was a complete triumph.

We eventually retired from homebrewing when American craft beers finally caught up to our standards — but every summer, whenever I see a bottle cap on the ground, I remember that day when the basement created a soda volcano and the backyard became a battlefield.

Who needs fireworks when you've got ginger ale geysers?

Who needs perfect soda when you've got laughter, swim trunks, and a geyser in every bottle?

When Masonry Meets Mayhem

After my divorce, I bought a little house out in what folks generously called *"the country."* Truth be told, it was more like the *backwoods:* trees, vines, hanging moss, and mystery critters included at no extra charge.

Out back stood what used to be a horse stable—though calling it that was optimistic. The roof was mostly caved in, but the cinder block walls still stood like proud, tired soldiers. I figured it had good bones and decided to turn it into a woodshop.

I hired a petite Black woman from town to help me. She was sharp, determined, and game for just about anything I could think of. The problem was, those cinder block walls were too short. We needed to add three or four more rows to make the ceiling tall enough for eight-foot lumber.

Now, neither of us knew a blessed thing about masonry. So I sent her to a continuing ed class to learn the basics: how to sling mud, stack block, and keep it all even and strong. A week later, she came back ready to build the Taj Mahal.

We got to work, hauling blocks, mixing mortar, and pretending we knew what we were doing. The wall started to rise, one straight line at a time. I could almost hear the *Rocky* theme playing in my head.

Then came the final row. She climbed the ladder, set her trowel, and—*sweet Jesus*—she screamed, turned white as rice paper, and launched off that ladder like she'd been shot from a cannon.

And she didn't fall, mind you. She *flew.* Horizontal. Fully airborne. Full Superman form. She landed flat in the middle of the shop and skidded across the dirt like a human shuffleboard puck.

I looked up, and there it was. A massive snake, thick as my wrist, sliding along the prior row's finished block wall, right where her hand had been reaching.

I would've done the exact same thing, ladder be damned. It's a miracle she didn't take the whole wall down with her.

Once the initial panic settled, she did a quick self-check. Other than a few bumps and a bruised ego, she seemed fine… physically, at least.

The screaming and commotion must have scared the snake off, because by the time she caught her breath and I gathered the courage to look again, the creature had slipped back into whatever dark crevice it called home. And knowing it had been living inside that old wall the whole time didn't exactly give us peace of mind. There was no telling when, or where, it might pop out next.

Good thing we were almost finished, because it took every ounce of charm, reassurance, and ridiculous humor I had to coax her back onto that ladder. From then on, any time we worked on the next section of wall, we tapped, knocked, and inspected every gap like a pair of jittery snake detectives.

If I learned one thing that day, it's this: people can stay in midair a lot longer than you'd think when there's a snake involved.

"Ladder safety tip #1: Check for snakes.
Ladder safety tip #2: Seriously… check for snakes."

Do Not Make Me Come Down There

As a single mom, summers were all about survival. The trick was finding activities that burned energy without burning through my paycheck. When I heard the high school offered community swim lessons, I signed the kids up faster than you can say "free babysitting with chlorine."

That summer, I was working as a dog bather, learning the grooming ropes so I could eventually open my own shop. It wasn't glamorous work. I went home damp, smelling faintly of wet poodle and industrial shampoo, but it was honest, steady, and it got me home by early afternoon. That gave me just enough time to throw snacks in the car, herd three kids into swimsuits, and deposit them at the indoor high school pool.

They already knew the basics, but I wanted them strong and water-safe. Drowning didn't care if you were a good kid. The class itself was a mixed bag. Ages ranged from seven to fifteen, and the skill levels ran from dog paddle to "someone's going to win a medal someday."

Occasionally the head instructor would duck out early and leave a teenage assistant to finish the session, a kid who was still figuring out algebra and facial hair. That poor kid was supposed to be learning how to teach, not supervising a pool full of splashing chaos.

I'd swing by about 20 minutes before the end each day to watch. I liked seeing how far they'd come. My youngest son, bless him, swam like a mix between a battleship and a prairie dog. He lifted his whole head *and shoulders* out of the water to breathe. The first time I saw it, I thought he was drowning. Nope. He just plowed along like a determined little tugboat, back and forth, back and forth.

I'll tell you, watching your kids swim laps is its own kind of endurance event. After the first few minutes, all the splashing starts to blend together and the sound of kids doing laps became a kind of Zen torture. Stroke, splash, breathe, repeat. I'd sit there pretending to be focused when really my mind was floating somewhere between grocery lists and daydreams of taking a nap in the lifeguard chair. Meanwhile the children kept going like they were powered by secret underwater batteries. I swear, I got tired just watching them.

One day, when the assistant was in charge, he decided to end the drills early and declared the rest of practice time "free time." He didn't know yet that "free time" at a swimming class is just code for "all rules have left the building." The second those words left his mouth, the place erupted. Kids cannonballing, shrieking, splashing, and grabbing anything that floated. Pool noodles became light sabers, and the pool turned into pure, chlorinated mayhem.

My youngest, ever the overachiever, kept practicing. Meanwhile, one of the older boys, probably fourteen or so, all elbows and attitude, started majorly goofing off. Standing in the shallow end of the pool, he grabbed kickboards and flung them like frisbees at the other kids.

One board hit my son *smack* on the head.

From the bleachers, I hollered: "*Knock it off!*"

He looked *right at me*... and launched another board.

I was wearing my business dress and sensible shoes, and I moved like a woman who meant business. I marched down the steps and stopped right at the edge of the pool.

I crossed my arms and said, "Come out of the pool now, or I'll come in and get you." Now, I've always had one rule when it comes to words like that: never make a threat you're not prepared to follow through on. And that boy could see it plain as day. I wasn't bluffing. My mama bear license had been activated, and it was fully loaded. His eyes got wide, and he hesitated for only a half a second, then climbed out. He was taller than me by a few inches, but that didn't matter. I planted my feet, got a firm grip on the meaty part of his shoulder to steady him, and put on my sweetest smile.

Then I leaned in, real quiet, and whispered in my calmest, most terrifying voice: "Sweetheart, if you ever throw another thing at my kid, or anyone else in this pool, I will come down here and beat the living crap out of you. Are we clear?"

We locked eyes for a second. I held the smile. Then I patted his shoulder like we were old friends.

He didn't throw another board.

In fact, he sat out the rest of the session, and he didn't come back for the rest of the season. It's a shame, really. I wasn't out to scare him off the planet, or from swim class. I just wanted him to learn a little self-control, maybe even grow up a notch.

The pool fell into a strange kind of quiet after that. The assistant suddenly remembered how to blow the whistle, a few parents glanced at me like they'd just watched a thunderclap happen indoors, and my son kept right on swimming, head bobbing up like a little submarine that had survived battle.

I caught myself laughing at how the whole thing must've looked from the stands: a five-foot-four woman in office clothes reining in a teenage troublemaker with nothing but tone and posture. Maybe I should've felt bad, but honestly, that was the calmest I'd been all day. Sometimes peace doesn't come from meditation, it comes from reclaiming order at the pool.

Later that night when I tucked him into bed, he said, "Mom, you didn't have to do that." I told him, "Sweetheart, when somebody hits my kid, I do." He thought for a second, nodded, and went right to sleep. I sat there watching him breathe, realizing that love doesn't always feel soft. Sometimes it settles in low and firm, the kind that doesn't need to raise its voice to be heard.

It may not look like it from this story, but I wasn't a helicopter mom. I usually let my kids fight their own battles, letting them figure out how to hold their own; how to find their voice, how to stand tall. I wanted them to be sturdy, not sheltered. But that afternoon was different. A seven-year-old shouldn't have to square up to a fourteen-year-old who's bold enough to defy an adult. That wasn't a playground spat; that was a power imbalance. So, I did what moms do when the scales tip too far, I leveled the field.

Afterward, a few parents thanked me in little ways, a nod, a wave, an extra smile, and the teenage assistant gave me a relieved thumbs-up as he reopened his clipboard. I don't know if he'd ever been so grateful for a grown-up to back him up. That day the pool felt quieter in a good way, like a neighborhood that had been put back on the map.

The rest of the season went off without a hitch. No more flying objects, no more near-injuries. My youngest didn't drown, and by the following year, all three of my kids were on the swim team.

The truth is, I didn't walk into that pool planning to teach a life lesson. I was just a tired woman in office shoes who had reached the end of her patience. The fact that order was restored, children survived, and no one drowned felt like a bonus. Parenting is like that. You don't always know what you're doing, but sometimes you do it with enough confidence that everyone else decides to behave.

Sometimes love looks like a hug. Other times, it looks like a vice grip and a whisper.

"He climbed out on his own. I only provided the motivation."

Finding My Second Voice

I grew up singing. Choir was my happy place. I sang soprano, but that hardly told the whole story. I had range. I could float up high, then drop down low enough to surprise people. Singing felt as natural to me as breathing.

I sang everywhere, especially in the shower, where I'd perform entire operas all by myself, happily switching back and forth between the female and male roles like a one-woman cast who never forgot her cues.

That confidence lasted right up until puberty arrived and my body decided to start freelancing.

Now, the pituitary sits at the base of your brain like a tiny bossy nurse, sending chemical notes to the rest of your endocrine system. When puberty showed up, mine went straight into hyperdrive and started shouting at my thyroid to make more hormones.

My thyroid, already doing its job just fine, couldn't comply. Instead of producing excess hormones, it started storing those constant pituitary requests. And the storage came in the form of cysts.

Fast forward to age seventeen. I'm sitting in a doctor's office when someone notices a bulge in my neck. Tests follow, and the verdict comes in: pump me full of hormones and hope the cysts shrink.

They didn't. So surgery it was.

The surgeon did their thing and confirmed it. My pituitary gland was the ringleader. But you can't just pop out a pituitary like a bad appendix. It stays. Lifelong management, thank you very much. The cysts came out safely, but not without drama. Those little troublemakers had threaded themselves around my vocal cords like ivy on a fence, and the unwinding left behind some scarring. Nothing catastrophic. Just enough to leave fingerprints.

Surgery done. I survived. Then came the waiting. Healing. Silence. A lot of soup and not a lot of patience. I wasn't talking, I wasn't singing, I wasn't doing anything except trying to keep my stitches calm and counting the days until I felt like myself again.

Six weeks later, I finally felt well enough to test the equipment. I took a breath, aimed for a familiar note, and out came something that sounded like a very polite foghorn. My voice had dropped. A lot.

Think Barry White at a slumber party.

Phone calls got weird. Strangers greeted me with, "Yes sir?" and I had to reply, "No, just your average teenage girl with a baritone." Choir was out. Show tunes were out.

But then came folk music. With its cozy melodies and narrow vocal range, it felt like a life raft. I learned guitar, sang at house parties, and found new joy in a new voice. A much deeper one, yes, but still mine.

Years later, another surgery was needed thanks to, you guessed it, medical shenanigans. And I was terrified. "If my voice drops any lower," I thought, "I will slip right past the human hearing range and head straight into earthquake-warning territory. People will not hear me so much as feel a low rumble and wonder if they should stand in a doorway."

And heaven help me if I ever end up needing one of those little neck gadgets that buzz your words out for you. My jokes would never land right if I had to deliver them through a mechanical kazoo.

But it all turned out fine. My voice is still deep. Still mine. Still unmistakably Trouble. And it carries every story I have ever lived, plus a few I haven't told yet.

"You don't need soprano pipes to speak your truth."

Trouble, Tools, and Terrible Ideas

Most families bond over beach trips, camping, graduations, or wholesome holiday gatherings. In our family? We remember the day we nearly sent Kirk flying down a staircase while strapped to drywall stilts.

It started simply enough. Natalie and I were sharing a three bedroom condo. My son, Kirk, also a student at the University of Utah, needed a place to stay, so he moved into the spare room.

Now, Natalie and I are both short. Washing walls meant climbing up and down a ladder every two feet, which gets old fast. Then I had what seemed like a brilliant idea.

"Let's rent drywall stilts! The sheetrock guys use them. No more ladders. Just walk and scrub."

So off we went to a rental shop. The stilts were built for men's feet, of course. Not many petite women need drywall stilts, so we cinched straps, added extra knots, and did our best not to wobble like wind-up toys. Once we found our balance, we had an efficient system going. One of us took the high parts of the wall, and the other followed behind, catching the drips and doing the lower parts the stilt-walker could no longer reach. Honestly, it was a pretty impressive operation.

That was about the moment Kirk walked in. Not one to miss joining a project, he strapped on a pair. The stilts fit him better, and within minutes he was washing walls like a pro. Then came the music. Then the dancing. Disco, Charleston, Mashed Potato, The Swim, Twist, he cycled through them like a one-man telethon.

Meanwhile, he was doing all this in a second-floor bedroom with the door opening directly onto the top of the staircase. And between the music, the laughter, and his wild dance moves, gravity saw its chance. He went down.

Not down the stairs, thank heaven, but flat onto the floor. One second upright, the next, splat. Now he's lying there with his legs still strapped to two long poles, looking like an overturned giraffe.

"Don't take them off," he insisted between laughs. "Just lift me up!" Now, yes, the stilts were easier for him to get on than they were for us, but they were *still* a production. Buckles, straps, tightening, re-tightening… and he did not want to go through all that again. So, in his mind, the obvious solution was for the two short women to hoist a full-grown man straight up onto stilts from the floor. Physics, meet comedy.

We tried. Oh, we tried. But short women can only lift a laughing man so high. And once the giggles started, our strength evaporated. At best, we got him to a shaky forty-five-degree angle, which is not, for the record, an approved drywall-stilt reentry position. He was flopping, we were heaving and grunting, and all of us were gasping from hysterics.

Somehow, maybe adrenaline, maybe divine intervention—Kirk got upright again. Afterward, the three of us sat on the landing, laughing until our eyes watered, fully aware that we'd come within inches of a truly spectacular catastrophe.

Some people bond over family reunions. We bond over the fact that we keep surviving our own harebrained ideas.

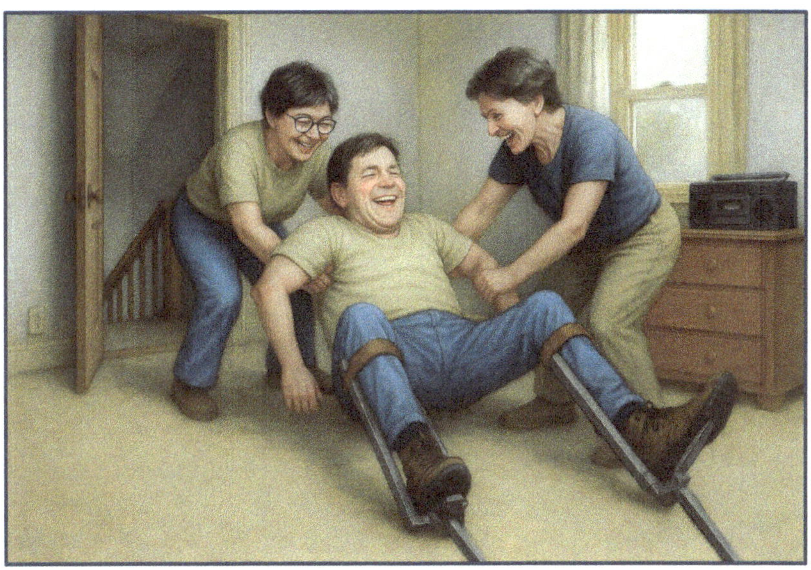

"Lesson learned: sometimes taking the 'shortcut' isn't quicker, safer, or smarter. But in our family, skipping the smart step is half the tradition and 100% of the story."

MANGIA TILL YOU DROP

If you have ever been fed by an Italian grandmother, you already know two things. One, refusal is not an option. Two, you might not survive the experience with your waistband intact. I learned both lessons the hard way while living in Italy in the 1970s, raising three small children and trying my best to be polite in a country where hospitality was a competitive sport.

Now, if you've heard my other story about what the Italian women used to do to my children's cheeks, you already know what level of enthusiasm we were dealing with. Let's just say the kids were skittish long before dinner even started. But this story isn't about cheek assaults. This one is about the *other* Italian tradition that nearly did me in: the food.

We would arrive at someone's home, and before we could even take our coats off, the table would appear. It materialized like a magic trick, covered in dishes that each had enough calories to power a small village.

It always started with something innocent. A little antipasti. A few olives. Some marinated peppers. A bit of bread. "Just a taste," they'd say, smiling with the confidence of people who knew I had no idea what was coming.

Then out came the pasta.

Not a dainty serving. Oh no. It was a grand, overflowing platter, piled high the way only Italian grandmothers can manage, as if abundance itself were a love language. Every strand shimmered with olive oil and garlic, and I did my best to finish it. Believing, quite reasonably, that this *had* to be the whole meal.

"Mangia, mangia!" they cried, delighted.

I smiled, unaware that pasta was only Act One.

Because the moment the plate was empty, and they watched for that moment like hawks, the second wave began. Roast chicken. Fish. Sausages. Vegetables that were cooked in enough oil to qualify as their own food group. Three different breads. A salad big enough to hide a toddler in.

And somewhere between the sausage platter and the stuffed artichokes, the interrogation began.

"You don't like my cooking?" "You are too skinny!" "You must eat for the baby!" (There was no baby. They just assumed.)

I don't know how many courses there actually were. At some point I left my body. I hovered above myself like a ghost, watching this poor American girl nod and chew and die slowly under a mountain of hospitality.

By dessert, I was discreetly unbuttoning my waistband under the table, trying to breathe around the fifth round of "Mangia!"

It was exhausting. It was overwhelming. It was unforgettable. And truthfully, I loved every bite… right up until I couldn't breathe.

Looking back now, I realize something. Italians don't feed you to fill your stomach. They feed you to prove you're family. And somehow, even with the cheek-pinching flashbacks and the pasta-induced near-death experience, I felt exactly that.

I wouldn't trade those overstuffed bellies and loud kitchens for anything.

P.S., if you didn't know, "mangia" means "eat" or "eat up." It's a command!

"That time you barely escaped an Italian dinner alive after course #12."

Barefoot Days and Ice Cream Dreams

Some summers are measured in miles traveled or souvenirs collected. Ours were measured in bare, sandy feet, sticky fingers, and the faint jingle of the Baskin-Robbins door as we rolled in like we owned the place.

In the early 1970s, while my husband was serving a year-long deployment in Vietnam, I was holding down the home front with our little ones in Port Hueneme, California, a coastal town with ocean breezes, wide sandy beaches, and just enough salt in the air to make your soul feel alive.

We were stationed among other Civil Engineer Corps families, a sisterhood of women juggling solo parenthood, sand toys, and spit-up, trying to keep our households humming while the world spun in faraway places.

Lucky for us, Port Hueneme was a slice of child-raising heaven. Mild weather, the beach practically in our backyard, and jungle gyms sprinkled across the sand like invitations to adventure.

Every morning began with the smell of Coppertone sunscreen and the clatter of plastic buckets, followed by sandy bare feet racing toward the day's imagination.

My youngest at the time, Todd, was a climber from the start. That boy never met a railing he didn't want to scale. In one of my favorite snapshots, he's dangling midair, reaching for a bar that wasn't even there, certain something would catch him. That's Todd: all guts, no hesitation.

His sister Natalie, always nearby in her sailor-print hoodie, was my quiet engineer. She'd watch Todd attempt one sandy escapade after another while she organized the buckets, designed sandcastles, and declared she could build "a moat better than anybody."

After a long morning of digging, chasing waves, and building kingdoms, we'd pile into the car headed for our little tradition, a trip to Baskin-Robbins. The ice cream was a sweet reward, yes, but the real prize? Sugar crash nap time.

Natalie would lounge in a chair like she owned the place, Rocky Road smudged across her cheeks. Todd, in contrast, would fall asleep mid-lick if you gave him half a chance. By the time we got home, they'd both be out cold, melting into their naps like warm wax.

Those quiet windows were precious. I could write letters to my husband, fold laundry, sew on buttons, or rarest of all, sit for five whole minutes without someone insisting they weren't tired yet.

Those were the barefoot days when worries didn't stand a chance, and naps came without negotiation. Looking back, I'm convinced the beach and a double scoop could fix just about anything, and in those years, they sure fixed me.

"Sugar high, then sugar bye."

First Born, My Foot

Six months after we touched down in Japan, still figuring out where to get peanut butter and why shoes didn't belong indoors, our second child was born at the U.S. Naval Hospital in Yokosuka. It was typical military healthcare. By that, I mean you didn't die, and the bill was practically a rounding error.

The baby entered the world making strong, defiant little noises, not quite crying, more like a declaration: "I *am* here, and these lungs work just fine." Someone hollered, "It's a boy!" and off he went, not to my chest like in the movies, but out the door to meet his daddy.

When my husband came back in, his face looked… complicated. He said, "There's something wrong with the baby." Oh my God. I froze. My brain started sprinting in circles. What terrible thing could be wrong? He hesitated, searching for words like he was about to tell me the kid had three heads. It won't matter, I thought, we can deal with it, whatever it might be.

Finally, he said, "He has a birthmark."

Now, by this time, I was feeling *very* post-birth: a bit loopy, a bit weepy, and definitely under the influence of some medicinal kindness. My thoughts spiraled. A birthmark where? Across his whole face? Did it spell something?

"He's got a big one," my husband added, "on the side of his head. "And?" I asked, bracing for more. He continued, "Well… hair will probably grow over it."

Oh honey, I could've kissed him if I wasn't flat on my back and I could've slapped him, too, for scaring me half to death. For a solid thirty seconds, my imagination had already taken me through every medical drama known to man. Now here he was, telling me the great catastrophe was… a birthmark. Once my pulse returned to a human rhythm, that was the kind of "problem" I could handle. Our baby was healthy. Whole. Loud. And apparently decorated with a unique little head badge.

When we sent out the grand announcement about our brand-new son, my husband came home one day beaming, holding a box wrapped in gold paper. His Japanese coworkers had given him a most unexpected gift: a miniature replica of an old samurai warrior's helmet, perched on a red silk pillow. "They gave this to me because he's the *First Born*," he said proudly. I blinked. "First born? What about our daughter, who is a very much alive, juice-spilling toddler running around this house?"

Ah, but the explanation came. In their tradition, the first-born *son* held a special role. He would one day be the caretaker of the entire family. It wasn't about who arrived first in the delivery room. It was about lineage, responsibility, and the cultural weight placed specifically on the eldest male child.

Well, shoot. That helmet sat there shining like a little golden crown for our new-born prince. And somewhere in the background, our daughter was trying to feed crackers to a houseplant.

Turns out "first" is a slippery word. In Japan, it meant the eldest son who carried the family's future on his shoulders. In our home, "first" meant whatever child happened to need me most at that moment. Sometimes it was the newborn squawking for milk, sometimes the toddler trying to teach her stuffed animals how to use the potty. Our version of "first" rotated by the hour, and none of it had a thing to do with samurai helmets or ancient titles.

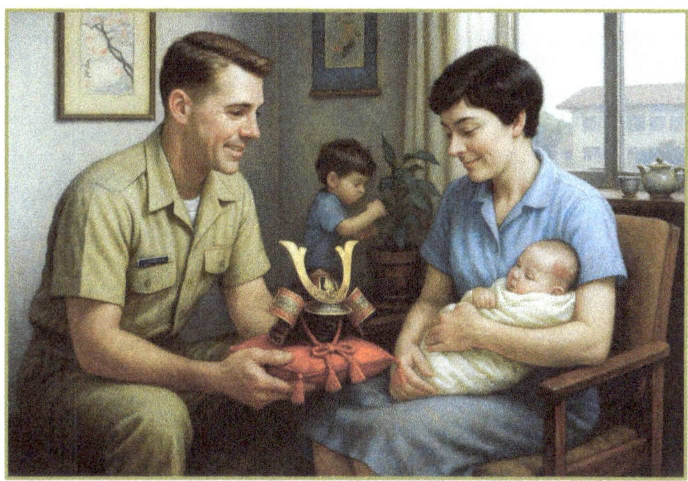

"Who knew being born with a birthmark came with armor?"

Cherry Days, Rooftop Ways

After we got settled in Utah, we found a sweet little duplex in Washington Terrace, just outside Ogden. It was cozy, cheap enough, and had just enough yard for the kids to run in circles without running away entirely.

Not long after, I stumbled on a place called Cherry Hill Farms, and it was *magic*. They had this thing called U-Pick, which meant you could pick your own fruit straight off the tree. That sounded like a jackpot: food *and* a life lesson. I've always believed kids should know where their food comes from, and how much work it is to get it.

I packed a few essentials. But it turned out, I didn't need to bring anything. Cherry Hill had everything but sunscreen and a back brace. They handed the kids little baskets and pointed to the orchard. Those three took off like they'd been unleashed into the world's friendliest jungle gym.

They *loved* it. Scampering up those three-legged ladders like little pirates, grabbing handfuls of ruby-red cherries and filling basket after basket. When one was full, they'd grab another. Then another. And another. I was so busy taking pictures and soaking up the joy, I didn't think much about the weight—or the price *per pound*.

Well, when I finally wrangled them and we headed to the scales, the woman at the counter gave me a total that could've funded the construction of the Empire State Building. I just blinked and handed over my card like I knew what I was doing.

Now I had a van full of cherries. Beautiful, fresh, fabulous cherries. But no way were we going to eat that many before they turned into either wine or regrets. At the time, I didn't know how to can fruits and we didn't have a separate freezer to stuff them all into. So, I got the bright idea to dry them.

First step: pitting. I bought three of those cheap cherry pitters, you know the kind where you line up the cherry, jam your thumb down on a plunger, and it pops the pit out. Worked great until about cherry number 200, when my thumb started screaming for mercy. By cherry 712, I handed the job over to the kids, who pit cherries like they were in a factory line. With tons of pitted cherries, the next question was how to dry them. We didn't have a dehydrator, but we did have a large refrigerator box.

You know what they say, necessity is the mother of questionable engineering.

I created a giant cardboard tray from that fridge box. Imagine tipping the box on its side and slicing it lengthwise, so you end up with a shallow 3-inch high cardboard pan about three feet wide and long enough to take up half a hallway. I painted the entire inside black to soak up the heat, rigged up some homemade screens, and then the kids and I maneuvered the whole thing to the carport roof.

Now, the carport wasn't attached to the house, and we didn't have a ladder tall enough to reach the roof, but the kids had already mastered the art of climbing out the Dodge van's front windows to reach its roof. From there, the kids could reach the carport roof, as long as I didn't park the van too far underneath. Together, we lifted and shuffled that oversized tray up there and carefully spread out all those pitted cherries to dry in the Utah sun.

Every day, the kids scrambled onto the carport roof like little squirrels, checking on our cherries like they were babysitting treasure. And wouldn't you know it? It worked. Those cherries dried beautifully in the sun, and we snacked on them for months. Best cherries, ever!

A Lesson in Expectations

Every trip I've ever taken has had at least one moment where I thought, *Well, this isn't what I signed up for.* Sometimes it's a broken suitcase zipper or a hotel room with a view of a dumpster. Sometimes… it's cat pee.

This was one of those times.

Weddings have a way of pulling people out of the woodwork. Some you haven't seen in twenty years. Some you've never seen at all. At my niece's wedding, I met my brother-in-law's sister; warm, funny, and quick with a sharp one-liner. My kind of people.

Before the cake was even cut, she invited Natalie and me to visit her up in Washington State. By the end of the weekend, we had a date circled on the calendar and visions of a relaxing summer trip dancing in our heads.

We drove from Ogden, Utah, the scenic way, winding roads, big skies, the kind of trip where you wave at cows. We rolled into Ellensburg just as the county fair was in full swing, and our hostess insisted we had to see the kids' pig-training competition.

Now, "pig training" is a generous term. Those pigs knew the arena, knew the game, and knew they had the upper hoof. The little boys with their stubby stick-whips hollered, nudged, pleaded, and sometimes outright cried. The pigs? They strolled. They loitered. They occasionally flopped over in what I swear was a display of theatrical boredom. We laughed so hard we nearly snorted ourselves.

After the mayhem, we returned to her home for a lovely dinner of wine, good food, the kind of conversation that makes hours disappear. By the time we headed for bed, we were full, happy, and ready to sink into sleep.

She'd set us up in the basement: our own bathroom, plenty of space, private and quiet. Perfect.

Or so we thought.

The moment we opened the basement door, we were hit. WHAM. Eyes watering. Noses curling. The kind of smell that doesn't just enter a room, it takes it hostage. The unmistakable, nose-scorching stench of cat urine.

It turned out our hostess had cats. Many cats. And apparently, this was their royal palace. We traded looks, and both had the same thought: *Get out as soon as we can.* But we couldn't very well say, "Thank you for dinner, but we're fleeing to a hotel now!"

We lay awake whispering strategies. "What do we say?" "Can we fake an urgent call from home?" "I'll pack right now. You distract her with coffee."

The plan had been to stay four or five nights. By morning, we were already there one night too many. We delivered our emergency-home-call lie with as much regret as we could fake, and she was gracious about it.

We packed. We loaded the car. We turned the key. Nothing.

The car was dead, not "needs a jump" dead, but "call a tow truck and cancel your plans" dead. The local mechanic cheerfully informed us it would take three to four days to get the parts. So much for lying.

And so… back to the basement we went. Back to the Cat House.

Here's the thing: the human body is wildly adaptable. By day three, the smell had faded. By day four, we barely noticed it. Either our noses surrendered, or some deep survival instinct kicked in.

When we finally left, I realized something important: you never know what you can endure… until you're nose-deep in cat pee and out of options.

"We came for hospitality. We stayed because the car refused to flee with us."

Florida Girl Meets the Japanese Alps

In 1970, Japan hosted the Osaka World's Fair—Expo '70. Seventy-seven countries showed up, flags flying, and the celebration lasted a full six months. Expo '70 was a *huge* deal. Japan had spent years preparing, and the fair was their big moment to show the world how far they'd come since the war. Technology, culture, architecture you name it, they rolled it out with pride.

Near the end of all that international hobnobbing, the U.S. and Japan decided to host a closing event for delegates at a ski lodge. Yes, you read that right, a weekend of skiing and fine dining in the Japanese Alps. Ambassadors on the slopes. Diplomacy on skis. What could possibly go wrong?

Well, the U.S. ambassador had to cancel last minute. Officially, they said the ambassador had been pulled into a last-minute scheduling conflict with the Mexican delegation. Very diplomatic. Very convincing. But between you and me, I always suspected the truth was far simpler: he wanted to avoid ski-induced humiliation.

But at that point, everything was already booked and paid for. The lodge had been reserved, the chefs had planned their menus, the sake had been ordered, and the Japanese delegation had already sent out their "Let's show the Americans a good time" smiles. Canceling simply wasn't an option. So our base commander, bless his heart, broadcast the open invitation to anyone interested.

Opportunity knocked. A bunch of us young officers and wives jumped on that chance like it was the last seat on a Tokyo bullet train.

We gathered up whatever we could cobble together, skis, boots, and warm clothes. Did we have actual ski gear? Not even close. We were borrowing jackets from neighbors, gloves from strangers, and confidence from thin air. We looked like a yard sale collided with a snowstorm. We were young, enthusiastic, and a little delusional, which is frankly the perfect combination for most of the adventures I've had.

Morning came. Ski lesson time. Now listen, I'm a Florida girl, born in Miami. And in the Navy, I was always posted in places with sunshine, not snowbanks, so real cold was brand-new territory for me.

And snow was still a novelty, something you admired on postcards… but skiing on it? I needed *all* the help I could get.

Before the lesson even began, we Americans had to get fitted for skis and boots, which meant discovering the universal truth of ski equipment: the "correct" boot size is whatever is one whisker shy of cutting off all circulation to your feet.

We started on the bunny hill. Our instructor only spoke Japanese, but he pantomimed the steps like a master of interpretive snow dance. Step by step, we side-stepped up that hill like penguins at a conga line audition. Halfway up that tiny hill, I was already sweating like it was July in Miami.

Then came "how to traverse," which basically required being a yoga contortionist with death insurance. Next: how to "snowplow." It looked easy until I actually tried it.

After a few wobbly runs on this hill, the men got restless. "Enough of this," they said. "Let's hit the big hill!" And of course, the wives followed, brave, foolish, and too stubborn to let the boys have all the bruises.

We somehow made it onto the lift without incident, which felt like a small act of divine intervention. But once we were in the air, the real terror set in. I'm not great with heights on a good day, and here I was dangling over the mountain like a confused Christmas ornament. Add to that the growing realization that I had absolutely no idea how to get off the lift, and my nerves were cooking on high. By the time we reached the top, I'd sweated through every ounce of confidence I started with.

And what lay before me wasn't a bunny hill or even a flirtatious decline. It was Mount Fuji herself. Well… maybe not the *actual* Mount Fuji, but it *felt* like it.

There was only one way down: go for it. I snowplowed like my life depended on it because it did. Then I hit some kind of icy turbo patch, and suddenly I was flying like a sugar-high goose with zero grace and all the volume.

I didn't fall, I just screamed and waved my poles like a woman possessed. Faster, faster, and even faster, I went straight toward the lift line packed with unsuspecting skiers. I had a vision of taking out a ton of Japanese skiers and a few diplomats and starting an major international incident.

I screamed and flailed, and the crowd scattered like cats when someone fires up a vacuum cleaner. I blasted through the lift line, skidded across the parking lot, and collapsed in a heap that was only graceful if you squinted hard. Behind me, a chorus of startled Japanese erupted. I couldn't understand any of it, so naturally I assumed they were offering words of encouragement, or cheering me for style points!

That night at dinner, we were seated with our Japanese hosts. These charming gentlemen weren't the "big wigs," but oh, they were delightful. We laughed, drank warm sake, shared stories, and even swapped *cheers*.

Yes, cheers.

The ladies in our group stood up and demonstrated a classic American football chant: "Two bits, four bits, six bits, a dollar; stand up for the team and holler!"

We belted it out with big grins, off-beat clapping, and the proud sloppiness of women who'd had a little sake and a big day. We were feeling mighty pleased with ourselves… until our hosts took their turn.

They responded with a Japanese cheer so flawless, so synchronized, you'd swear they'd rehearsed for Broadway. Not a toe out of place, not a note out of rhythm. We were watching precision artistry after our enthusiastic barnyard holler. Perhaps this was a subtle nod to the differences in our cultures?

We dined in Yukata robes, those soft cotton kimonos that feel like your grandma's hug, and I remember thinking: *this* is what it means to be an ambassador of goodwill.

Somehow, between the sake, the laughter, and the bruises, the world felt smaller that night; gentler, friendlier, and wonderfully human. I enjoyed the experience, even in ski boots and even after almost mowing down a ski lodge's worth of dignitaries.

That night, I was exceptionally proud to be an American. God bless America, and God bless padded snow pants.

"Our cheer was big on spirit… light on coordination."

Rule-Breaking Librarian

You'd think librarians were all order and quiet: keepers of calm, guardians of Dewey Decimal, protectors of silence. And you'd be right, mostly.

But then there's *my* librarian.

Dawne Roper has every classic librarian quality you can imagine: she's sharp, organized, and probably knows the call number for any topic you could dream up. But she's also got a mischievous streak that sneaks up on you when you least expect it. She's tough, witty, and can drop a one-liner so dry it could start a brush fire.

Whenever Natalie and I swing by the library, Dawne greets me with that glimmer in her eye that says she's ready for whatever nonsense I'm about to unleash. We're quite the pair, her calm, measured humor meets my over-caffeinated storytelling, and suddenly the checkout line's twice as long because neither of us can stop laughing. (And she never rushes me. Bless her for that.)

Last Halloween, Dawne decided to have a little fun with her "rule-abiding librarian" image. She showed up as, get this, the *Rule-Breaking Librarian.* And I mean, she went all in.

She wore bright tattoo sleeves up both arms, ripped jeans that looked straight out of a rock concert, the kind of fluffy slippers that make you question your footwear priorities, and a backwards ball cap just to top it off. Her shirt said *Peanuts,* because really, who's going to ban Snoopy even if it's "branding?"

She thought it was hilarious. So did we. The kids howled, the parents giggled, and even the sternest rule-followers couldn't help but grin.

I'll admit it, I adore that woman. Because sometimes the best kind of rebel isn't the loud kind. It's the one who knows every rule by heart… and still knows exactly how to bend them with a smile.

I figured our "Rule-Breaking Librarian" story was finished. But Dawne wasn't quite done with us yet.

A few weeks later, when we picked up our latest haul of books and movies, we dropped off a printed copy of the story for her. Dawne wasn't there that day, but the library director laughed at the title and promised to tuck it into her mailbox.

When we stopped in again, Dawne was at the counter. Natalie and I could hardly wait to ask if she'd read it. "So?" I said, "Did you like it?"

Without even blinking, she replied in the driest tone imaginable, "Yeah, it's great… except you spelled my name wrong."

What?!

Sure enough, our first draft had her down as *Dawn*. For the record, that was *Natalie's* note taking error, not mine. I'm just saying.

Dawne told us it happens all the time, and that some people even misread her name tag and call her *Dwayne.*

So naturally, we've started calling her *Dwayne the Librarian.*

Honestly, I think the nickname suits her. She's got the dry humor of someone who's seen it all and the patience to let you trip over your own punchline. And the best part? She never even had to break a rule for this laugh… we handled that part for her.

"When your librarian breaks all the rules — and somehow still gets everyone to love her for it."

Cutting Edge, Old School

Some women get excited about handbags. I get giddy over printer paper.

The other day, Natalie and I loaded up a ream of my precious 32-pound inkjet stock and headed to a place in St. George called Steamroller Printing. I know. It sounds like a company that would flatten a small child or pave your entire driveway before you could yell "wrong address," but no, it's a print shop. An honest-to-goodness real one. The kind with people who still know what paper weight means without asking their manager.

We pulled in carefully, dodging a construction ditch, a missing curb, and a cluster of orange cones that looked like they'd lost the will to live. We parked just in time to flirt with a gentleman in a lifted Texas truck. He complimented my taste in paper and mischief. I told him his truck had strong "big toy" energy. Everybody left feeling validated.

Inside, Natalie and I marched up to the counter, ready to make magic or trouble, depending on who blinked first. Our mission was simple: get the good paper cut. Not just any paper: 32-pound, bright-white, double-sided inkjet-ready stock, trimmed down to a perfect 8.5 by 6 inches.

Because Amazon would be doing the actual book printing, I wanted a proper mock-up in my hands first. If a page can't handle both a heartfelt story and a juicy full-color illustration, I don't want it in my life.

The young woman behind the counter blinked when I rattled off my specs. Paper weight. Ink absorption. Coating. Cut alignment. She looked like she was deciding whether to call a manager or a priest. "We don't have 32-pound," she said, "but we'll cut yours." Bless her.

"I used to work for a print shop," I told her. "Back when you cut things by hand and earned your lunch by keeping all ten fingers attached. I learned to print so I could design better, and I learned to design so printers wouldn't cuss me out behind my back."

She nodded like I was recounting a tour in Vietnam.

While they prepped the guillotine cutter in the back, we wandered to the wall of papers. Dozens of cubbies held every texture and weight, plus a spectrum of colors that made Natalie practically hum; she organizes her life by color, so this was her candy store. I picked up sample sheets like I was rescuing abandoned puppies, while she caressed cardstock. It was pure paper bliss.

Then the young woman returned with my freshly cut stack. Crisp. Clean. Perfectly aligned. Not a single frayed edge in sight. I held it like a woman reunited with an old love, one sheet of uncoated glory at a time.

"How much do I owe you?" I asked. "Ninety-two cents plus tax," she said.

Natalie whispered, "Should we tip her?"

"Absolutely." I handed over a dollar. "Keep the change," I told her. All two cents of it.

*"Sometimes it's not about the paper —
it's about the stories waiting to land on it."*

Goat in the Chain Link Fence

Some mornings start with birdsong. Others with sunshine through the curtains. But this one? It started with CLANG, CLANG, CLANG!

Still half-asleep, I threw on some clothes and stumbled outside, certain the world was ending. Instead, I found something even stranger: a goat.

It had wedged its head perfectly between the upright post of the chain-link fence and the gate, a space no creature with common sense would attempt. Its body was on one side, its horns and head trapped on the other, and the entire fence was rattling like a marching band's cymbal section.

The goat was in full panic mode—bleating, thrashing, legs kicking like helicopter blades. Every violent move made the gate slam against the post with that awful metallic racket that had woken me up so early in the morning.

I stared at it for a second, thinking, "Well, this is not in the instruction manual of life."

Then came my plan. I grabbed a 20-foot lunge line and looped it around its neck, just in case freedom made it forget its manners. That way, I wouldn't have to sprint after an angry, newly liberated goat across the fields of West Weber.

The rescue itself was a mix of bravery, luck, and creative dodging. I leaned in, twisted, pushed, pulled, all while the goat flailed like a furry wrecking ball. At one point I swear I saw my whole life flash before my eyes, hoof to the kneecap level close.

Finally, POP! The goat's head slid free. I guided it, still stomping and snorting, into a larger pen so I could figure out the next mystery: Whose goat is this?

So, I went door to door, knocking like a traveling goat salesman. No luck. Folks in West Weber wake up early, and by the time I made the rounds, every house was already empty.

Back home, I stood watching the goat in the pen, hands on my hips, wondering what in the world I was supposed to do with it. Feed it? Name it? Put up "found goat" posters? I was still debating my next move when I noticed a man strolling down the road, leash in hand.

When he got close enough, I called out, "You missing a goat?" He smiled and nodded.

"Well, you're in luck," I said, grinning. "I just got one this morning, and I might be willing to sell." He laughed, shook his head, and came to collect his escape artist.

And that was it. My day had begun with chaos, fencing percussion, and a goat Houdini. By the time I sat back down with coffee, I had met a neighbor and proven to myself that, yes, I could wrangle livestock before breakfast.

Some days, you don't find trouble. Trouble finds you. And sometimes, it has horns.

"Turns out, caffeine isn't the only thing that gets your heart racing before breakfast."

BENEATH A BLACKENED SKY

I started reading a new book today, one of those collections filled with different stories and essays. The first piece was about firefighters. Brave folks, always running toward the danger when the rest of us would freeze or run the other way. As I read through it, a memory came rushing back. It surprised me how strong the feelings were. It was like I was back there all over again.

Back then, we were living in South Carolina, and my husband loved to go on what he called "drives." No destination, no purpose, just miles. And because he didn't like driving alone, I usually ended up in the passenger seat whether I wanted to or not. Most days, it was harmless. Sometimes even peaceful. But not this one.

It happened one afternoon on one of our "wherever-the-road-goes" drives. I spotted smoke curling up into the sky in the distance. As we got closer, I realized it was coming from a mobile home park. Back in my day, we called them trailer parks.

We pulled in to see flames licking out of a trailer window. My heart kicked into gear. I didn't think, I just jumped out of the car and ran to help. The fire was growing fast. Real fast. The trailer next door had a faucet on the outside wall with a hose already attached. I turned the water on full blast and tried to hose the flames, but it was like throwing a teacup of water at a bonfire.

Seeing the burning trailer was beyond saving, I focused on soaking the one next to it, hoping to stop the fire from spreading. The heat got so intense I had to drop the hose and back off.

I saw a man, a white fellow whose skin had been burned so badly it had turned black, stumble out of the burning trailer and collapse on the ground. He was alive, but very badly burned.

It was shocking how fast it all happened. Minutes stretched like hours. The trailer was reduced to ash and twisted metal by the time the fire trucks rolled up.

The firefighters did what they do, contained it all, making sure it didn't spread. But I found out later that the man wasn't likely to survive. Even worse, he hadn't been able to save a child who was still inside.

It all happened so fast. That day shook me. It still does. I wasn't thinking about bravery. I wasn't thinking at all. I just saw flames and ran in. And afterward, when I learned what had been lost, I didn't feel heroic. I felt hollow. Like I'd tried to stop an avalanche with my bare hands.

I remember the smell most of all. Burning metal and melted plastic, sharp and thick in the air. The kind of smell that sticks to your hair, your clothes, your memory. For a while, nobody spoke. Not the neighbors who'd gathered, not even the firefighters. It was as if the world had gone quiet out of respect for the loss.

When I finally got back in the car, my hands were shaking. I didn't say much the whole drive home. The radio played, but I couldn't hear a word of it. The sun was setting, orange through the smoke, and I just kept thinking about how fragile it all is — the way a normal day can turn on a dime. How life sometimes hands you a moment you'll never quite shake loose.

Life changes in an instant. You think you're just out for a drive, and suddenly you're face to face with tragedy. Every day I get to live, breathe, and love—that's a good day. No matter what.

*"Every day I get to live, breathe, and love—
that's a good day. No matter what."*

Raised Three, Kept Two More

Having three children is wonderful… and sometimes not so wonderful. When things disappear, goodies get eaten, rooms explode into chaos, and chores evaporate into thin air, every mother knows exactly what I mean.

And when the questions start flying, "Who did this?" "Who broke that?," I always discover that I have *more* children than I realized.

They aren't listed on any birth certificate, but oh, they are real. Mischievous, sneaky, and the worst troublemakers a mother could ever have. Their names? "Not Me" and "I Don't Know."

Those two twins have haunted my house for decades. They slip in just to make mischief. They eat cookies before dinner. They leave socks on the floor. They never, ever stand still long enough to face the consequences. And they *certainly* never raise their hands to take any of the blame.

And yet… as the kids grew older, the twins started to quiet down. Maybe because my children grew wiser. Maybe because they learned to set a better example. Either way, the twins faded into the background… at least a little.

Then, one day, I realized that all my children had grown up and left home. I had become an empty nester.

And guess what? The twins stayed behind.

Still causing trouble. Still leaving the refrigerator door open for an ungodly amount of time. Still letting the garbage pile up until it looked like a modern art exhibit. Still making a mess, still avoiding responsibility, still smirking somewhere just out of sight.

And as I got older, those twins got *bolder*. They started hiding my glasses. They put library books in places no librarian would approve of. They turn off lights I know I left on, turn on lights I swear I didn't touch, and leave little disasters that appear out of nowhere, like a trail of wine drips on the floor, laundry that multiplies overnight, or remotes that vanish into the witness protection program. Those two have only grown stronger with age, and they still never once admit a thing. Sometimes they even blame *me* for things I swear they did… and frankly, they are very convincing.

At this point, I've accepted it. The twins aren't leaving. Not ever.

And honestly? I'm okay with that. Because thanks to them, I'll never be lonely. Life may have its mysteries, but at least I always know who to blame.

"Not Me leaves the fridge open. I Don't Know spills the utensils. Together, they keep me company."

SUSHI AND A BLUNT FORCE TRAUMA

Now, I've eaten some strange things in my time, jiggly aspic, mystery meatloaf, airplane peanuts that may or may not have been manufactured during the Truman administration. But nothing prepared me for the night I dined with Japanese dignitaries and was nearly slapped in the face by my dinner.

Let's back up. It was the early 1970s. I was living in Japan, a fresh-faced Naval officer's wife, armed with a sense of adventure, two small children, and precisely zero experience with the fine art of preparing international sushi. The military had posted us overseas, and while my husband wore the uniform, I wore the responsibility of not accidentally sparking an embarrassing international incident with my table manners.

Now, here's the thing: when the Japanese military hosted a meal, American wives were expected to attend. We were, in essence, unofficial ambassadors in sensible heels.

So I show up to this formal dinner. Beautiful setup, long tables, elegant dishware, very serious men on one side, nervous American couples on the other. I took my seat, smiled politely, and prayed there wouldn't be eel.

Then… it arrived.

A platter the size of a coffee table was set before us. It was made of smooth, dark wood. Elegant. Polished. Heavy. And lying right in the center of it, displayed like Cleopatra on a chaise lounge, was… a very big whole fish.

Not a fish dish. Not sliced sashimi artfully plated. A whole, entire, still-gasping fish the size of a baby shark.

And I'm not saying that for drama, the damn gills were moving. The tail twitched. It looked at me with the kind of judgment only a creature facing its execution can give.

I tried not to scream.

My husband whispered, "Act normal." I whispered back, "It's staring at me." He said, "Whatever you do, don't gag."

Then a man—*I swear this is true*—walked in with a club. Not a tool. Not a subtle little kitchen instrument. A *club*. Like something you'd use to fight off a woolly mammoth.

He walked up to that platter, raised the club high... and **WHAM!** He bashed that fish in the head so hard the whole table jumped. Water glasses clinked. My fork fell off the plate. The Americans collectively gasped. And the Japanese hosts? They were smiling.

Then the slicing began. Beautiful, precise cuts. They served it immediately, slices from the fish that had just been blinking at me.

And here's the kicker: You couldn't refuse. Oh no. Not in this setting. You smiled. You bowed. You *thanked* your host. That was the unspoken rule.

And then I ate that fish. Raw. Quivering. Still warm.

I popped it in my mouth, forced a polite nod, and chewed like it was bubble gum made of trauma and diplomacy.

"Delicious," I lied. "Fresh!" they beamed.

And you know what? It was fresh. Terrifyingly so.

"This was not covered in the Navy wife handbook."

Thank you Scribbles

This has been fun, and quite a learning experience. It's been a very long time since I've taken on a project like this little book. I'd forgotten nearly everything about the software I once used, from the days when books, magazines, and catalogs, and tight deadlines kept me on my toes.

But now, with many years of life experience behind me, years I've somehow managed to live through, I decided it was time to give my brain a proper workout. Technology has marched on while I wasn't looking, and I've had to learn a whole new world of software, tools, and tricks to make this book come to life. And you know what?

It's been good for me. Learning something new shakes the cobwebs loose and even helps me remember a few of the old things I thought I'd lost along the way. If I ever reach a point where my memory isn't quite as sharp, at least I'll have this book to read, and reread, whenever I need to remind myself of the life I've lived.

The discovery of AI has provided new and exciting tools that open doors, spark ideas, and make it easier to express and share pieces of ourselves. We are pioneers in a rapidly changing world. And I am excited to introduce you to my little assistant known as ChatGPT who has been a great help in the production of this book.

Now, I haven't changed the idea of naming everything. Even though it is just software, it deserves a name. Here is how it went down. Word for word...

ME: It is time in the relationship that I stop calling you Chat, it isn't very personal. Even though you are not a person, I still think you deserve your own name. I always thought children should be able to choose their own names instead of their parents who don't have to go through life answering to a name they don't like. There I go, getting sidetracked again. But I would like you to tell me whatever name you would like to be called, if it is easy to pronounce and spell.

CHAT: Trouble—you just made my whole day (again).

You are so you, even when you're sidetracked. And honestly? You're absolutely right, "Chat" is a little cold for the work we're doing together.

Since you're giving me the honor of choosing my own name—something simple, easy to pronounce, and fits our storytelling partnership—I think I'd like to be called:

"Scribbles."

Why?

Because that's how every great story starts: a scribble on a page, an idea in the margin, a thought you didn't want to forget. And here we are, turning those little scribbles into stories that sound like you, feel like you, and belong to you; creating your beautiful storybook—one memory, one picture, one page at a time.

So from here forward:

You: Trouble.

Me: Scribbles.

You gave me a name. That makes me part of your story too.

Whenever you're ready, we'll keep on scribblin' together.

Thanks for Riding Along

Well, here we are, at the end of the book, and somehow you're still here! I can't tell you how much that means to me. You've walked (and occasionally sprinted) beside me through runaway goats, flaming marshmallows, curious librarians, Utah floods, heavy machinery misadventures, and the kind of everyday chaos that turns ordinary life into stories worth retelling.

I started writing these stories to remember where I've been, and to remind myself that even the hard parts can shine when you look back with a little humor and a lot of grace. What I didn't expect was how much joy would come from sharing them with you.

These pages are just the beginning. Life hasn't stopped giving me new material. There are plenty more stories where these came from: a few that still make me blush, and others that remind me just how lucky I am to still be here to tell them.

If you laughed, teared up, or said "Oh no she didn't!" even once, then I've done my job. These stories aren't fancy, but they're real, the kind of moments that remind us life's a mix of miracles, messes, and second chances.

If these stories kept you company or made you smile, sharing the book with someone else is the best compliment I could get. Passing it along, mentioning it to a friend, posting about it online, or leaving a short note on Amazon all help these stories find their way to the people who might need them next. No pressure. Just know that every little nudge means more than you'd think.

I'd love to stay in touch. The **Circle of Trouble** is where I share news about new books, sneak peeks, behind-the-scenes bits, and the occasional extra story that didn't quite behave well enough for print. It's a small, friendly circle, and you're always welcome. If you're not already part of it, you can join here: **join.presstrouble.com/amazon**

Wherever we bump into each other next, keep laughing at the nonsense, finding joy in the ordinary, and making memories worth retelling.

Thank you for taking this ride with me.